As of May 17, 2012, this guidance applies to federal savings associations in addition to national banks.*

I0455208

Comptroller of the Currency
Administrator of National Banks

Bank Supervision Process

Comptroller's Handbook

September 2007

*References in this guidance to national banks or banks generally should be read to include federal savings associations (FSA). If statutes, regulations, or other OCC guidance is referenced herein, please consult those sources to determine applicability to FSAs. If you have questions about how to apply this guidance, please contact your OCC supervisory office.

Bank Supervision Process

Contents

Introduction

Background

The Office of the Comptroller of the Currency (OCC) is responsible for the oversight and supervision of the national banking system. In carrying out its mission, the OCC seeks to assure a banking system in which national banks

- Soundly manage their risks,
- Maintain the ability to compete effectively with other providers of financial services,
- Meet the needs of their communities for credit and financial services,
- Comply with laws and regulations, and
- Provide fair access to financial services and fair treatment of their customers.

This booklet explains the OCC's philosophy and methods for supervising national banks.[1] It focuses on the entire supervisory process for all types of banks.[2] This booklet integrates general supervisory policy for safety and soundness and specialty areas and includes in the appendix a consolidated reference for all uniform interagency rating systems. It also outlines bank supervision responsibilities and addresses how the OCC coordinates its supervision with other banking and functional regulators.[3] Additionally, this booklet explains how the OCC's quality management programs, customer assistance group, and appeals process support bank supervision.

Philosophy

The OCC employs a risk-based supervisory philosophy focused on evaluating risk, identifying material and emerging problems, and ensuring that individual banks take corrective action before problems compromise their safety and soundness. This philosophy is embodied in the OCC's supervision by risk program. The OCC carries out risk-based supervision for safety and soundness purposes, including specialty areas such as consumer compliance, asset management, and information technology.

To consistently integrate risk-based supervision into all aspects of the supervisory process, the OCC has implemented a supervisory framework consisting of the following three components:

---

[1] For the purposes of this booklet, the terms "national bank" and "bank" include any national banking association and any federal branch or agency of a foreign bank, and their operating subsidiaries, unless specifically excepted.

[2] Although the "Large Bank Supervision," "Community Bank Supervision," and "Federal Branches and Agencies Supervision" booklets provide details for supervising those banks, this booklet represents the central reference for bank supervision policy.

[3] Functional regulators are those non-banking regulators who have primary supervisory responsibility for functional lines of business (e.g., securities, commodities, or insurance activities) conducted in a bank, its subsidiaries, or affiliates. Refer to "Functional Regulation" for more information.

- **Core Knowledge**—the OCC's database that contains core information about the institution, its profile, culture, risk tolerance, operations and environment, and key examination indicators and findings. This database enables examiners to document and communicate critical data with greater consistency and efficiency.

- **Core Assessment**—objectives and procedures that guide examiners in reaching conclusions on both risk assessments and regulatory ratings. Examiners must reach these conclusions during the course of each supervisory cycle to meet the requirements of a full-scope, on-site examination. Specific core assessment guidance is contained in the "Large Bank Supervision," the "Community Bank Supervision," and the "Federal Branches and Agencies Supervision" booklets, and the Core Examination Overview and Procedures sections of the FFIEC *Bank Secrecy Act/Anti-Money Laundering (BSA/AML) Examination Manual*. (Updated 9/28/2012)

- **Expanded Procedures**—detailed guidance that explains how to examine specialized activities or specific products that warrant extra attention beyond the core assessment. These procedures are found in other booklets of the *Comptroller's Handbook*, the FFIEC *BSA/AML Examination Manual*, and the FFIEC *Information Technology (IT) Examination Handbook*. Examiners determine which expanded procedures to use, if any, during examination planning or after drawing preliminary conclusions during the core assessment. (Updated 9/28/2012)

High-quality supervision is essential to the OCC's ability to carry out its mission. As defined by the agency, high-quality bank supervision

- Is dynamic, responsive to changing risks at individual institutions, and sensitive to evolving market conditions and regulatory changes.

- Reflects the unique characteristics of each bank, including size and risk profile, and establishes minimum supervisory assessment standards.

- Ensures that banks have appropriate risk management systems that encompass a sound audit program and a strong internal control system.

- Recognizes the role of functional regulators and promotes effective coordination with them.

- Ensures that examiners recognize and appropriately assess the risks posed by all significant lines of business, including those subject to the primary supervision of another regulator.

- Ensures that banks comply with laws and regulations and adhere to safe and sound banking practices.

- Is based on clear communication of bankers' and examiners' responsibilities.

- Uses OCC resources efficiently and effectively by allocating the greatest resources to the areas of highest risk.

- Is performed by supervisory personnel who have the knowledge and skills to accurately evaluate a bank's condition, identify risks, and communicate effectively with bank personnel, the OCC, and other banking and functional regulators, as appropriate.

Types of Banks

For supervisory purposes, the OCC designates each national bank as a **large**, **mid-size**, or **community bank**. This designation is based on the bank's asset size and whether other special factors that affect its risk profile and complexity are present or absent, such as:

- The bank and its affiliate national charters are part of a much larger banking organization (company) and proper supervision requires extensive coordination with other regulators.
- The company is a dominant player within its market.
- The company has large asset management operations.
- The company performs significant international activities.
- The company owns unique operating subsidiaries.
- The company offers high-risk products and services.
- The company conducts sophisticated capital markets activities.

Affiliates–Because many national banks are a part of diversified financial organizations, the OCC assesses the risks to these banks posed by related entities to the extent necessary to reach conclusions about the consolidated organization. This approach recognizes that risks present in a national bank may be mitigated or increased by activities in an affiliate.

To differentiate national bank affiliates, the OCC uses the terms "lead national bank," "significant national bank affiliate," and "smaller national bank affiliate." The "lead" national bank is the national bank affiliate with the most assets, unless the company designates another national bank. A "significant" national bank affiliate has assets of $1 billion or more. A "smaller" national bank affiliate has assets of less than $1 billion.

The OCC's supervisory process for community banks is detailed in the "Community Bank Supervision" booklet. The supervisory process for large and mid-size banks is detailed in the "Large Bank Supervision" booklet.

Federal Branches and Agencies

Federal branches and agencies are offices of foreign banking organizations licensed by the OCC to conduct banking business in the United States. Because of the global aspect and complexity of their operations, federal branches and agencies, regardless of size, follow large bank supervision policy. However, some aspects of their supervision are patterned on community bank supervision. Refer to the "Federal Branches and Agencies Supervision" booklet for more information.

Trust Banks

National banks that limit their services to fiduciary powers and incidental activities are referred to as national trust banks (NTBs). While most NTBs are not insured by the Federal Deposit Insurance Corporation (FDIC), deposit insurance may be available. An NTB is exempt from the definition of "bank" in the Bank Holding Company Act (12 USC 1841(c)(2)(D)), provided it meets certain conditions. Accordingly, some NTBs are independent, stand-alone entities, while others are subsidiaries of, or affiliated with, commercial banks, bank holding companies, financial service companies, or other business enterprises.

NTBs are generally designated as community, mid-size, or large banks, based on their affiliation with other financial institutions, volume of assets under management or administration, and complexity of operations.

Credit Card Banks

A national credit card bank is customarily either (1) a bank that engages exclusively or predominantly in credit card activities and that is owned directly by a bank holding company or an organizing group or (2) a CEBA (Competitive Equality Banking Act of 1987) credit card bank that is owned by a nonbank holding company, commercial entity, or a bank. The first type of bank may legally offer additional commercial banking services, such as deposit accounts for its employees, unless prohibited by its articles of association. The second type of bank must qualify for the exemption created by the CEBA amendment to the Bank Holding Company Act (12 USC 1841(c)(2)(F)). All credit card banks are FDIC insured.

Because of their unique operations and risk profiles, credit card banks are categorized separately to facilitate common supervision, unless the bank has been designated a large bank or is an affiliate of a large bank.

Other Special Purpose Banks

Other special purpose banks, such as community development banks, bankers' banks, and banks that limit their activities to cash management, are designated as community, mid-size, or large banks based on asset size and the risk factors described previously. Refer to the "Charters" booklet of the *Comptroller's Licensing Manual* for more information on special purpose banks.

Bank Supervision Responsibilities

The OCC is organized in a manner designed to most effectively supervise the different types of national banks. Large banks are centrally supervised through the OCC headquarters office in Washington, D.C. by Deputy Comptrollers under the Senior Deputy Comptroller for Large Bank Supervision. Mid-size and credit card banks are supervised by Assistant Deputy

Comptrollers (ADCs) under the oversight of the Deputy Comptroller for Mid-size and Credit Card Banks. Community banks, federal branches and agencies, and trust banks are supervised by ADCs under the oversight of the district Deputy Comptrollers. The district Deputy Comptrollers and the Deputy Comptroller for Mid-size and Credit Card Banks report to the Senior Deputy Comptroller for Mid-size and Community Bank Supervision in Washington, D.C.

Supervision is an ongoing process in all types of national banks. Ongoing supervision includes monitoring activities, assessing risks, completing core assessments, and communicating with bank management and directors throughout the supervisory cycle. The OCC achieves ongoing supervision in large banks by having a staff of examiners on-site throughout the year. In mid-size and community banks, ongoing supervision assists the supervisory office in strategy development and resource allocation by creating flexibility in scheduling.

Portfolio Manager/Mid-Size and Large Bank EICs

To facilitate ongoing and consistent supervision, the OCC assigns responsibility for each national bank to a **commissioned national bank examiner**.[4] The OCC terminology for these examiners varies according to the type of bank they are supervising. In community banks and federal branches and agencies, these commissioned examiners are referred to as "portfolio managers" because they often are responsible for the supervision of several institutions. In large and mid-size banks, the commissioned examiner assigned supervisory responsibility is the "examiner-in-charge" (EIC). The large bank or mid-size bank EIC is responsible for the supervision of all national bank affiliates within the company. Personnel selected for these assignments are rotated periodically to ensure that their supervisory perspective remains objective.[5] Whether an examiner supervises a single company or a portfolio of banks, the supervisory responsibilities are consistent.

The portfolio manager/EIC

- Maintains an up-to-date understanding of the risks of each assigned bank or company.

- Identifies risks and responds in an appropriate and expedient manner.

- Considers the risks posed by each significant line of business within the bank or company, including lines subject to the primary supervision of another regulator, in determining the bank's ratings and consolidated risk assessment. The portfolio manager/EIC is not involved in the day-to-day supervision of a line of business that is supervised by another functional regulator. However, he or she should obtain information to determine the risks posed by those lines of business and how effective the bank's risk management systems are in controlling those risks.

---

[4] The appropriate ADC may assign supervisory responsibility to a noncommissioned examiner who is appropriately supervised by a commissioned examiner or the ADC.
[5] Examiners should refer to PPM 5000-38 (Revised), "Large Bank EIC Rotation."

- Maintains responsibility for ongoing supervision and ensures that examination plans are carried out throughout the supervisory cycle according to OCC standards. The portfolio manager/EIC must obtain approval from the supervisory office to change examination activities outlined in the supervisory strategy and must document the rationale for such changes in the OCC's supervisory information systems.

- Updates OCC's supervisory information systems to reflect the current risk profile and condition of a bank. When consolidated supervisory strategies are used, the portfolio manager/EIC ensures that the electronic files of affiliated national banks are cross-referenced.

- Maintains ongoing and effective communication with bank management and the board of directors.

- Keeps the supervisory office informed about the status of assigned banks.

- Establishes and maintains points of contact with both domestic and foreign banking supervisors and other regulatory agencies (such as the Securities Exchange Commission), consistent with the company's corporate structure and lines of business as discussed in the "Functional Regulation" and "Planning" sections of this booklet. Examiners should work with these points of contact to supervise the consolidated entity by facilitating the exchange of necessary information, coordinating supervisory activities, and communicating critical issues to the appropriate regulator.

- Implements OCC and supervisory office directives.

- Recommends to appropriate OCC management supervisory strategies (including enforcement actions) for the bank (and the consolidated company, if a mid-size or large bank) based on the nature of supervisory concerns, if any, the condition and risk profile of the bank, and the ability and willingness of the bank's management and board of directors to correct problems. If the portfolio manager/EIC has concerns about activities subject to the primary supervision of another regulator, he or she should contact the appropriate Deputy Comptroller to coordinate the supervisory response.

- Follows up on bank management's actions to address deficiencies noted during any supervisory activity.

- Follows up on any enforcement action involving an assigned bank by determining whether the bank is in compliance with the action and by assessing the effectiveness of bank management in correcting the problems.[6]

---

[6] Refer to "Enforcement Actions" for more information.

Examiner-in-Charge

In community banks, the examiner-in-charge (EIC) is the examiner assigned to conduct an examination. The EIC may be the bank's portfolio manager, another commissioned examiner, or a noncommissioned examiner appropriately supervised in an "acting" capacity. Appointing an EIC other than the portfolio manager can help examiners develop skills, use OCC resources more effectively, and distribute the workload more efficiently.

When a noncommissioned examiner serves as an acting EIC, his or her work must be supervised by a commissioned examiner or ADC who

- Reviews the accuracy of the acting EIC's work before findings are communicated to management.

- Attends the management exit meeting and board meeting to ensure consistent and effective communication.

- Signs the report of examination.

In large and mid-size banks, the OCC may also designate "functional" EICs to conduct examinations of particular areas or functions of a bank or company.[7]

Assistant Deputy Comptroller

An Assistant Deputy Comptroller (ADC) oversees the supervision of a portfolio of community banks, mid-size banks, federal branches and agencies, credit card banks, trust banks, or independent data centers. The ADC

- Maintains an understanding of risks within his or her assigned portfolio of banks, as well as an awareness of trends within the banking industry and financial services marketplace.

- Approves appropriate strategies for individual banks, ensuring that the banks address supervisory concerns, follow plans for corrective action, meet reporting requirements, and respond properly to enforcement actions.

- Supervises personnel who are directly responsible for bank supervision and facilitates the enhancement of expertise needed to supervise their assigned portfolio.

- Directs planning, scheduling, and monitoring of supervisory activities to ensure

    - Effective use of resources,
    - Consistency with identified priorities, and
    - Compliance with OCC standards.

---

[7] Functional EICs should not be confused with functional regulation, which is described elsewhere in this booklet.

- Assigns banks or groups of banks to appropriate personnel for periodic monitoring.

- Reviews the accuracy of the EIC's overall examination conclusions before findings are communicated to management.

- Ensures that the OCC's supervisory information systems reflect the current risk profiles and conditions of assigned banks.

- Attends management exit meetings and board meetings to ensure consistent and effective communication. ADCs may appoint designees to attend exit and board meetings, as appropriate.

- Maintains communication with points of contact at other regulatory agencies and coordinates requests from other regulatory agencies, both foreign and domestic, through the appropriate Deputy Comptroller. If another agency will participate jointly in an examination, the ADC communicates the overall scope to the portfolio manager or EIC so unnecessary duplication can be avoided.

- Countersigns reports of examination.

Supervisory Office

The OCC supervisory office supports and oversees the portfolio manager/EIC. Depending on the bank's size, condition, and risk profile, the supervisory office can be the field office, district office, or national office. Personnel who carry out these support and oversight responsibilities include supervisory office staff and either

- An ADC, if the bank is assigned to a field office or district office, or if it is a mid-size or credit card bank,

- The Deputy Comptroller for Special Supervision, if the institution is a problem bank assigned to the national office, or

- A Deputy Comptroller for Large Bank Supervision, if the bank is a large bank.

The supervisory office

- Maintains overall responsibility for and knowledge of the banks within its jurisdiction.

- Evaluates and approves the EIC's recommendations, including regulatory ratings and risk assessments.

- Evaluates and approves recommended corrective actions and initiates appropriate enforcement actions based on those recommendations.

- Communicates with the appropriate Deputy Comptroller regarding concerns about activities subject to the primary supervision of another regulator.

- Facilitates the exchange of information with other regulators through the appropriate Deputy Comptroller to ensure that portfolio managers/EICs are apprised of critical issues.

- Documents decisions concerning the supervision of the bank.

- Approves the supervisory strategy for each bank, ensuring that strategies are updated as needed.

- Ensures that scheduling of examinations for all banks meets statutory requirements.

- Works with portfolio managers, EICs, and other OCC management counterparts to ensure coordination of activities and priorities.

- Approves requests for participation in examinations with other regulators and communicates with portfolio managers/EICs to ensure coordination.

Regulatory Ratings

The OCC and other federal bank and thrift regulatory agencies use the uniform interagency rating systems adopted by the Federal Financial Institutions Examination Council (FFIEC) to assign ratings to an institution.

CAMELS

A bank's composite rating under Uniform Financial Institutions Rating System (UFIRS) or "CAMELS" integrates ratings from six component areas: Capital adequacy, Asset quality, Management, Earnings, Liquidity, and Sensitivity to market risk. Evaluations of the component areas take into consideration the institution's size and sophistication, the nature and complexity of its activities, and its risk profile.

Composite and component ratings range from **1** to **5**. A **1** is the highest rating and represents the least supervisory concern, indicating the strongest performance and risk management practices relative to the institution's size, complexity, and risk profile. A **5** is the lowest rating and represents the greatest supervisory concern, indicating the most critically deficient level of performance and inadequate risk management practices relative to the institution's size, complexity, and risk profile.[8]

---

[8] The CAMELS ratings definitions are in appendix A.

Specialty Area Ratings

Ratings are assigned for the specialty areas of information technology (IT), trust, consumer compliance, and Community Reinvestment Act (CRA). Consumer compliance, IT, and trust are rated 1 to 5. The CRA rating is descriptive rather than numerical.[9]

ROCA

Each federal branch and agency receives a composite rating under "ROCA." This rating of the institution's overall condition integrates the ratings of four areas: Risk management, Operational controls, Compliance, and Asset quality. Like CAMELS, the composite and component ratings for ROCA range from 1 to 5.[10]

Disclosure of Ratings

For all national banks, the CAMELS or ROCA composite and component ratings, and all applicable specialty area ratings, are formally communicated to the bank's board of directors and management through the Report of Examination (ROE) or other written communication.[11]

Examinations

The OCC examines national banks pursuant to the authority conferred by 12 USC 481 and the requirements of 12 USC 1820(d). These requirements establish minimum frequencies and scopes for examinations, known as the "supervisory cycle."

Examination Frequency

The frequency of on-site examinations of insured depository institutions is prescribed by 12 USC 1820(d). The OCC applies this statutory examination requirement to all types of national banks, regardless of FDIC-insured status, in 12 CFR 4.6.[12] **National banks must receive a full-scope, on-site examination at least once during each 12-month period.** The OCC may extend this requirement to 18 months if the following conditions are satisfied:

- The bank has total assets of less than $500 million;

- The bank is well capitalized as defined in 12 CFR 6;

- At its most recent examination, the OCC:

---

[9] Specialty area ratings are detailed in appendixes B, C, D, and E.

[10] The standards for evaluating and assigning ROCA ratings are in appendix F.

[11] Guidelines for disclosure of ratings are in appendix G.

[12] Note that the examination frequency for federal branches and agencies is prescribed by 12 USC 3105(c) and 12 CFR 4.7. Also, there are special considerations when applying the supervisory cycle to new charters and converted banks, and certain bank activities, such as CRA, have separate statutory examination frequencies.

- Assigned the bank a rating of 1 or 2 for management under the Uniform Financial Institutions Rating System (UFIRS), and

- Assigned the bank a composite rating of 1 or 2 under the UFIRS;

• The bank currently is not subject to a formal enforcement proceeding or order by the FDIC, OCC, or Federal Reserve System; and

• No person acquired control of the bank during the preceding 12-month period in which a full-scope, on-site examination would have been required but for this exception.

The statutory requirement sets a **maximum** amount of time between full-scope, on-site examinations. OCC supervisory offices may schedule examinations more frequently under certain circumstances—for example, when potential or actual deterioration requires prompt attention, when a change in control of the institution has taken place, or when there is a supervisory office scheduling conflict. Before increasing the frequency of examinations, supervisory offices should consider how OCC resources can be used most efficiently and how heavy the burden will be on the bank.

New Charters and Converted Banks

The examination frequencies prescribed by 12 USC 1820(d) apply to newly chartered (de novo) banks and banks that have newly converted to a national charter. Initially, de novo banks must receive a full-scope, on-site examination within 12 months of commencing operations. A de novo bank will remain on a 12-month examination cycle until it

• Has had two full-scope, on-site examinations;

• Achieves stability with regard to earnings, core business operations, and management; and

• Meets other criteria for extending the cycle as described previously.

A converted national bank must receive a full-scope, on-site examination within 12 months from

• The date of its last full-scope examination by a federal banking agency (FDIC, Office of Thrift Supervision (OTS), or Federal Reserve Board), or

• The date of its last examination by a state regulator, if the examination met Federal Financial Institutions Examination Council guidelines.

This time period may be extended to 18 months if the converted bank meets the standard statutory criteria for such an extension.

Because de novo and converted banks may initially present higher risk profiles and unique supervisory challenges, more intensive monitoring and closer supervision are prudent during their initial years of operations as national banks. Examiners should refer to Policy and Procedures Manual (PPM) 5400-9 (Revised), "De Novo and Converted Banks," for additional guidance. (This document is OCC internal policy and is not available to banks.)

Federal Branches and Agencies

The examination frequency for federal branches and agencies is prescribed by 12 USC 3105(c)(1) and further refined in 12 CFR 4.7. Like national banks, federal branches and agencies must receive a full-scope, on-site examination at least once during each 12-month period. The 12-month period may be extended to 18 months if the federal branch or agency

- Has total assets of less than $500 million;

- Has received a composite ROCA rating of 1 or 2 at its most recent examination;

- Satisfies either of the following:

  - The foreign bank's most recently reported capital position is at least 6 percent for Tier 1 and 10 percent for total risk-based capital on a consolidated basis; or
  - The branch or agency has maintained eligible assets on a daily basis, over the past three quarters, of not less than 108 percent of the preceding quarter's average third-party liabilities, and sufficient liquidity is available to meet obligations to third parties;

- Is not subject to a formal enforcement action or order by the Federal Reserve Board, the FDIC, or the OCC; and

- Has not experienced a change in control during the preceding 12-month period in which a full-scope, on-site examination would have been required but for this exception.

The OCC may also consider other discretionary factors, consistent with existing rules, in determining whether a federal branch or agency is eligible for an 18-month cycle.

Examination Types

Full-Scope, On-Site Examinations

The "full-scope, on-site examination" required by 12 CFR 4.6 and 4.7 is defined by the OCC as examination activities performed during the supervisory cycle that

- Are sufficient in scope to assign or confirm a bank's CAMELS or ROCA composite and component ratings, and specialty area ratings except CRA;

- Satisfy the core assessment;[13]

- Result in conclusions about a bank's risk profile;

- Include on-site supervisory activities; and

- Generally conclude with the issuance of a report of examination (ROE).[14]

Targeted Examinations

A targeted examination is any examination that does not fulfill all of the requirements of the statutory full-scope, on-site examination. The OCC sometimes combines several targeted examinations to accomplish the full-scope examination requirements. Targeted examinations may focus on one particular product (e.g., credit cards), function (e.g., audit), or risk (e.g., credit risk) or may cover specialty areas (e.g., municipal securities dealers).

There are also examinations that are conducted as part of OCC's licensing function, such as charter field investigations, pre-opening examinations, and conversion examinations. Refer to the *Comptroller's Licensing Manual* and PPM 5400-9 (Revised), "De Novo and Converted Banks," for additional information on these examination types. (The PPM is OCC internal policy and is not available to banks.)

Specialty Area Considerations

Specialty areas include information technology, asset management, Bank Secrecy Act/anti-money laundering (BSA/AML), consumer compliance, Community Reinvestment Act, and municipal and government securities dealers. The OCC generally conducts examinations of specialty areas as part of the full scope, onsite examination, following the principles of supervision by risk. However, in some areas the examination frequency and scope are influenced by statutory mandates or interagency commitments. (Updated 9/28/2012)

Information Technology Examinations

Information technology (IT) examinations are integrated within the 12- or 18-month supervisory strategy for all national banks. The level of expertise needed to perform the IT examination will typically depend on the bank's complexity and level of risk. IT examinations of community banks are usually performed by generalist commissioned and pre-commissioned examiners as part of the core assessment. More complex mid-size and large bank IT examinations are performed by bank information technology specialists using the procedures in the FFIEC *IT Examination Handbook.*

---

[13] For specific core assessment guidance, see the "Large Bank Supervision," the "Community Bank Supervision," and the "Federal Branches and Agencies Supervision" booklets, and the Core Examination Overview and Procedures sections of the FFIEC *BSA/AML Examination Manual.*

[14] Refer to the "Written Communication" section and appendix I for information on the ROE.

The OCC also conducts examinations of companies that provide IT services to national banks based on the authority granted by 12 USC 1867(c). These technology service providers (TSPs) include independent data centers, bank service corporations, joint ventures, and limited liability corporations. Some of these organizations are examined as part of the Multi-regional Data Processing Servicer (MDPS) program that is administered by the FFIEC IT Subcommittee of the Task Force on Supervision. The subcommittee selects companies for the MDPS program based on their systemic risk to the banking industry.

All TSPs are examined on a 24-, 36-, or 48-month cycle based on the Examination Priority Ranking Program described in the "Supervision of Technology Service Providers" booklet of the FFIEC *IT Examination Handbook.* Additionally, at least one interim review is required between regularly scheduled examinations.

Asset Management Examinations

Asset management includes trust and fiduciary activities, fiduciary-related services, transfer agent activities, and retail brokerage. The scope of the asset management review is based on the EIC's assessment of risk from asset management activities. In community banks with integrated supervisory strategies, examiners normally review applicable asset management activities as part of the core assessment. Refer to the "Large Bank Supervision," "Community Bank Supervision," and "Asset Management" booklets of the *Comptroller's Handbook* for additional guidance on supervising asset management activities.

Bank Secrecy Act/Anti-Money Laundering Examinations

12 USC 1818(s)(2)(A) requires the OCC to include a review of the BSA compliance program at each examination it conducts of an insured depository institution.[15] In addition, the scoping and planning process should ensure the examination includes compliance with Office of Foreign Assets Control (OFAC) legislation. The scope of the review in all banks shall include the minimum procedures in the Core Examination Overview and Procedures sections of the FFIEC *BSA/AML Examination Manual*, plus any additional core or expanded procedures that the EIC deems appropriate. Transaction testing must be performed at each review and should be risk-based. OFAC violations and MRAs must be reported to the Compliance Policy Division for referral to OFAC. (Updated 9/28/2012)

Consumer Compliance Examinations

Consumer compliance encompasses four functional areas of consumer protection laws and regulations—fair lending, lending (including the Flood Disaster Protection Act), deposits, and other consumer protection regulations. (Updated 9/28/2012)

For banks of all sizes, supervisory strategies for consumer compliance should be risk-based. In community banks with integrated supervisory strategies, examiners normally perform

---

[15] Section 1813(c)(3) provides that the term "insured depository institution" includes any uninsured branch or agency of a foreign bank or a commercial lending company owned or controlled by a foreign bank for purposes of section 1818 of this title. (Updated 9/28/2012)

consumer compliance examinations as part of the core assessment. The extent of transaction testing should reflect the bank's compliance risk profile, audit coverage and results, and the time elapsed since the last testing.

In large banks, the scope of the consumer compliance examination includes a review of the bank's compliance risk management system and can be focused on product lines and decision centers that carry the most risk.

During each supervisory cycle, examiners perform a fair lending risk assessment in each national bank. Based on the risk assessment, examiners may initiate appropriate supervisory activities to ensure compliance with fair lending laws and regulations. The OCC also identifies banks for comprehensive fair lending examinations using a screening process and a random sample that supplements the on-going supervisory office assessments. The screening process uses Home Mortgage Disclosure Act (HMDA) and other data.

As part of each full scope, onsite examination, the OCC must determine whether the insured depository institution is complying with the requirements of the national flood insurance program as mandated by 12 USC 1820(i). The risk-based evaluation should review any audit of the bank's flood protection program and conduct transaction testing of a sample of mortgage files if the audit does not include transaction testing.

Community Reinvestment Act Examinations

The Gramm–Leach–Bliley Act (GLBA) modified the CRA examination cycles for banks with total assets of $250 million or less. For these banks, which are on "extended examination cycles" because they are small, the minimum period between CRA examinations is 60 months if the bank is rated outstanding and 48 months if it is rated satisfactory. CRA examinations for banks with total assets of $250 million or less and an overall CRA rating of

- *Outstanding* at the most recent CRA examination ordinarily will start no sooner than 60 months, but no later than 78 months, following the close date [16] of the most recent CRA examination. The 60-month time frame is statutorily mandated, while the 78-month time frame is based on OCC policy.

- *Satisfactory* at the most recent CRA examination ordinarily will start no sooner than 48 months, but no later than 66 months, following the close date of the most recent CRA examination. The 48-month time frame is statutorily mandated, while the 66-month time frame is based on OCC policy.

- *Needs to improve or substantial noncompliance* will be based on a risk analysis of the particular bank and ordinarily will begin within 36 months from the close date of the most recent CRA examination. There are no statutory "extended examination cycles" for

---

[16] Close date is the supervisory office approval date.

banks with ratings of needs to improve or substantial noncompliance. The 36-month time frame is based on OCC policy.

Banks with total assets of $250 million or less that are rated outstanding or satisfactory may be examined more or less frequently than the GLBA-mandated "extended examination cycle" for reasonable cause, after consultation with and approval by the supervisory office's Deputy Comptroller.

The CRA examination cycle for banks with assets in excess of $250 million at the most recent CRA examination is based on the risk characteristics of each bank. Ordinarily, examinations will start within 36 months from the close date of the most recent CRA examination. Per OCC policy, the first CRA examination for a de novo bank ordinarily will be no sooner than 24 months and no later than 36 months after the bank opens for business.[17]

ADCs and large bank EICs may defer a CRA examination for up to one year beyond the due date. The appropriate Deputy Comptroller must concur on all deferrals exceeding one year and must notify the Deputy Comptroller for Compliance Policy of the deferral. The supervisory office records should contain brief documentation to support any deferral.

Municipal and Government Securities Dealers Examinations

The OCC is required by statute (Section 15B(c)(7) of the Securities Exchange Act of 1934, 15 USC 78o-4(c)(7)) to examine national banks that operate as municipal securities dealers. While the statute does not define the full-scope of the review, it does require that the OCC examine for compliance with the standards of the Municipal Securities Rulemaking Board (MSRB). Under MSRB Rule G-16, this examination must take place once every two calendar years. All other activities of the bank dealer are examined according to the safety and soundness standards set by the Federal Deposit Insurance Corporation Improvement Act of 1991 and OCC policy.

Under Section 15C(d)(1) of the Securities Exchange Act of 1934, 15 USC 78o-5(d)(1), all records of a national bank that operates as a government securities broker or dealer are subject to reasonable periodic, special, or other examinations by the OCC. When the OCC examines government securities dealers, its policy is to use the same specifications on scope and frequency that it does for municipal securities dealers. Such a policy is efficient because most government securities dealers are also municipal securities dealers.

Functional Regulation

The Gramm–Leach–Bliley Act of 1999 (GLBA) codified the concept of "functional regulation," recognizing the role of the state insurance commissioners, the Securities and Exchange Commission (SEC), and the Commodities Futures Trading Commission (CFTC) as the primary regulators of insurance, securities, and commodities activities, respectively.

---

[17] Examiners should refer to PPM 5400-9 (Revised) for guidance on scheduling CRA examinations at de novo and converted banks.

GLBA also reaffirmed the OCC's role as the primary regulator of national banks and its responsibility for assessing a bank's consolidated risk profile. This responsibility includes determining the potential material risks posed to the bank by functionally regulated activities. A key component of this assessment is evaluating a national bank's systems for monitoring and controlling risks posed by functionally regulated activities conducted by the bank or the bank's functionally regulated affiliates (FRAs). An FRA is a bank affiliate, including a bank subsidiary, whose primary regulator is a state insurance commissioner, the SEC, or the CFTC.

To assess the risks posed to the bank by its activities, the OCC uses a risk assessment process that is consistent with GLBA's functional regulation requirements. The assessment is integrated into the OCC's normal supervisory process and embraces the supervision by risk approach in determining the necessity, frequency, and depth of the analysis.

When assessing risk at individual national banks, the OCC must adhere to GLBA requirements that limit the agency's authority to require reports from an FRA, directly examine an FRA, impose capital requirements on an FRA, or take other direct or indirect actions with respect to an FRA. If the risk assessment identifies potential significant risk to the bank from an FRA's activities, the OCC must first request information from the bank or the appropriate functional regulator. If the information received from those sources is insufficient to assess the risks the FRA poses to the bank, the OCC may request from the FRA the information necessary to assess

- Whether a material risk to the affiliated national bank exists,

- The effectiveness of the system for monitoring and controlling operational and financial risks that may pose a threat to the safety and soundness of the affiliated national bank, or

- Compliance with federal laws that the OCC has specific jurisdiction to enforce against the FRA.

The OCC may directly examine an FRA only when the OCC

- Has reasonable cause to believe that the FRA is engaged in activities that pose a material risk to the affiliated national bank,

- Determines, through a review of relevant reports, that an examination of the FRA is necessary to adequately inform the OCC of the system for monitoring and controlling operational and financial risks that may pose a threat to the safety and soundness of the affiliated national bank, or

- Has reasonable cause to believe, based on reports and other available information, that the FRA is not in compliance with federal laws that the OCC has specific jurisdiction to enforce against the FRA. This includes provisions relating to transactions with affiliates when the OCC is unable to evaluate compliance through examination of the national bank.

Examiners should consult with, and obtain approval from, the appropriate Deputy Comptroller before requesting information from, or conducting an examination of, an FRA. The same protocol should be followed in the event a functional regulator invites an examiner to participate in a joint examination of an FRA.

Functional regulation requires reliance on the functional regulator for supervising the FRA and cooperation among all regulators in sharing information, as appropriate.[18] GLBA does not restrict the OCC from seeking information on an FRA from the bank or from sources other than the FRA to the extent needed to evaluate the risk the FRA poses to the bank.

GLBA limitations on the OCC's authority to require reports, conduct examinations, and take other actions do not apply when insurance, securities, and commodities activities are conducted directly in the bank, in another affiliate that is not an FRA, or through the bank's arrangements with unaffiliated third parties.[19] In these instances, the functional regulator is responsible for regulating the particular activity under its jurisdiction. The OCC may have supervisory authority over the activity for safety and soundness reasons, or based on separate statutory authority.

Supervision by Risk

Supervision by risk requires examiners to determine how certain existing or emerging issues for a bank, its related organizations, or the banking industry as a whole affect the nature and extent of risks in that institution. Supervision by risk guides examiners in the risk evaluation process by providing consistent definitions of risk, a four-dimensional system for assessing these risks (known as the Risk Assessment System or RAS), and integration of risk assessment in the supervisory process. Following risk evaluations, examiners tailor supervisory activities to the risks identified. Examiners must include periodic testing in supervisory activities to validate their risk assessments.

While the OCC's supervision focuses on individual banks, the risks to these institutions may be mitigated or increased by the activities of affiliates and other related organizations (e.g., financial subsidiaries). Therefore, examiners must determine the risk profile of the consolidated company, regardless of how activities are structured within the company. To do this, examiners obtain information from the bank, affiliates, and other regulatory agencies, as necessary, and verify transactions flowing between the bank and affiliates.[20]

---

[18] The OCC has entered into information-sharing agreements with most state banking and insurance departments. Examiners can reference these agreements on the OCCnet under "Legal."

[19] The OCC may exercise its authority under 12 USC 1867(c) to examine a third-party service provider. Examiners should seek information from the bank, and, if necessary, the functional regulator, before exercising this authority. These sources of information may eliminate the need to conduct a direct examination of the service provider.

[20] For additional information see "Functional Regulation."

The OCC's supervision concentrates on systemic risks and institutions that pose the greatest risk to the banking system. Under this approach, the OCC allocates greater resources to areas of higher risk. It does so by

- Identifying risk using common definitions. The categories of risk, as they are defined, are the foundation for supervisory activities.

- Measuring risk using common methods of evaluation. Risk cannot always be quantified in dollars. For example, numerous or significant internal control deficiencies may indicate excessive operational risk. (Updated 5/06/2013)

- Evaluating risk management to determine whether bank systems adequately identify, measure, monitor, and control risk.

- Performing examinations based on the core assessment or other expanded procedures, reaching conclusions on risk profile and condition, and following up on areas of concern.

Banking Risks

From a supervisory perspective, risk is the potential that events, expected or unexpected, will have an adverse effect on a bank's earnings, capital, or franchise or enterprise value. The OCC has defined eight categories of risk for bank supervision purposes: credit, interest rate, liquidity, price, operational, compliance, strategic, and reputation.[21] These categories are not mutually exclusive. Any product or service may expose a bank to multiple risks. Risks also may be interdependent and may be positively or negatively correlated. Examiners should be aware of this interdependence and assess the effect in a consistent and inclusive manner. Examiners also should be alert to concentrations that can significantly elevate risk. Concentrations can accumulate within and across products, business lines, geographic areas, countries, and legal entities. (Updated 5/06/2013)

The presence of risk is not necessarily reason for supervisory concern. Examiners determine whether the risks a bank assumes are warranted by assessing whether the risks are effectively managed, consistent with safe and sound banking practices. Generally, a risk is effectively managed when it is identified, understood, measured, monitored, and controlled as part of a deliberate risk/reward strategy, known as risk appetite. A bank should have the capacity to readily withstand the financial distress that such a risk, in isolation or in combination with other risks, could cause. (Updated 5/06/2013)

If examiners determine that a risk is unwarranted (i.e., not effectively managed or backed by adequate capital to support the activity), they must communicate to management and the board of directors the need to mitigate or eliminate the excessive risk. Appropriate actions may include reducing exposures, increasing capital, and strengthening risk management practices. (Updated 5/06/2013)

---

[21] The risk definitions are found in appendix H, "Categories of Risk."

Risk Management

Because market conditions and company structures vary, no single risk management system works for all banks or companies. The sophistication of risk management systems should be proportionate to the risks present and the size and complexity of an institution. As an organization grows more diverse and complex, the sophistication of its risk management must keep pace.

Large and mid-size banks. The risks that large and mid-size banks assume are often varied and complex, because of their typically diversified business lines and geographies. Thus, risk management systems of larger banks must be sufficiently comprehensive to enable senior management to identify and manage the risk throughout the company. Examinations of large and mid-size banks focus on the overall integrity and effectiveness of risk management systems. Annual validation, a vital component of large and mid-size bank examinations, verifies the integrity of these risk management systems.

Community banks. While risks historically have been concentrated in traditional banking products and services, community banks today offer a wide array of new and complex products and services. Therefore, risk management systems in community banks will vary in accordance with the complexity and volume of risk a bank assumes. Examinations of community banks focus on a bank's practices and its ability to properly manage risk. Using core assessments of these practices, OCC examiners draw conclusions about the adequacy of the bank's risk management systems. When risks are high; when activities, products, and services are more complex; or when significant issues or problems are identified, examiners will expand the scope of their supervisory activities to ensure that bank management has appropriately identified, measured, monitored, and controlled risk. The extent of the additional supervisory activities will vary based on the impact those activities, products, services, or significant issues may have on the overall risk profile or condition of the bank.

Regardless of a bank's size and complexity, sound risk management systems should

- *Identify risk*—To properly identify risks, a bank must recognize and understand existing risks and risks that may arise from new business initiatives, including risks that originate in nonbank subsidiaries and affiliates, and those that arise from external market forces, or regulatory or statutory changes. Risk identification should be a continuing process and should occur at both the transaction and portfolio levels.

- *Measure risk*—Accurate and timely measurement of risks is essential to effective risk management systems. A bank that does not have a risk measurement system has limited ability to control or monitor risk levels. Further, more sophisticated measurement tools are needed as the complexity of the risk increases. A bank should periodically test to make sure that the measurement tools it uses are accurate. Sound risk measurement systems assess the risks of both individual transactions and portfolios.

- *Monitor risk*—Banks should monitor risk levels to ensure timely review of risk positions and exceptions. Monitoring reports should be timely, accurate, and informative and should be distributed to appropriate individuals to ensure action, when needed. For a large, complex company, monitoring is essential to ensure that management's decisions are implemented for all geographies, products, and related entities.

- *Control risk*—Banks should establish and communicate risk limits through policies, standards, and procedures that define responsibility and authority. These limits should serve as a means to control exposures to the various risks associated with the bank's activities. The limits should be tools that management can adjust when conditions or risk tolerances change. Banks should also have a process to authorize and document exceptions or changes to risk limits when warranted.

The board must establish the bank's strategic direction and risk tolerances. In carrying out these responsibilities, the board should approve policies that set operational standards and risk limits. Well-designed monitoring systems will allow the board to hold management accountable for operating within established tolerances.

Capable management and appropriate staffing are essential to effective risk management. Bank management is responsible for the implementation, integrity, and maintenance of risk management systems. Management must

- Keep directors adequately informed about risk-taking activities.
- Implement the bank's or company's strategy.
- Develop policies that define the institution's risk tolerance and ensure that they are compatible with strategic goals.
- Ensure that strategic direction and risk tolerances are effectively communicated and adhered to throughout the organization.
- Oversee the development and maintenance of management information systems to ensure that information is timely, accurate, and pertinent.

Retaining and recruiting capable executives, line managers, risk management personnel, and back-office staff can be challenging in today's competitive job market. The skills and expertise of management and staff must be commensurate with the products and services the bank offers its customers. The skills required for larger institutions (and what a bank must pay the personnel who have them) are generally greater and more varied than those required in less diversified and complex institutions. Mergers and consolidation also present complicated personnel challenges. Merger plans should lay out strategies for retaining the staff members essential to effective risk management.

When examiners assess risk management systems, they consider the bank's policies, processes, personnel, and control systems. If any of these areas is deficient, so is the bank's risk management.

Policies are statements of actions adopted by a bank to pursue certain objectives. Policies often set standards (on risk tolerances, for example) and should be consistent with the bank's underlying mission, values, and principles. A policy review should always be triggered when the bank's objectives or standards change. (Updated 5/06/2013)

Processes are the procedures, programs, and practices that impose order on a bank's pursuit of its objectives. Processes define how daily activities are carried out. Effective processes are consistent with the underlying policies and are governed by appropriate checks and balances (such as internal controls). (Updated 5/06/2013)

Personnel are the bank staff and managers who execute or oversee processes. Personnel should be qualified and competent, and should perform appropriately. They should understand the bank's mission, values, principles, policies, and processes. Banks should design compensation programs to attract, develop, and retain qualified personnel. In addition, compensation programs should be structured in a manner that encourages strong risk management practices. (Updated 5/06/2013)

Control systems are the functions (such as internal and external audits, risk review, and quality assurance) and information systems that bank managers use to measure performance, make decisions about risk, and assess the effectiveness of processes. Control functions should have clear reporting lines, adequate resources, and appropriate authority. Management information systems should provide timely, accurate, and relevant feedback. (Updated 5/06/2013)

Risk Assessment System

The OCC's risk assessment system (RAS) provides a consistent means of measuring risk and determining when examiners should expand the examination scope. The RAS is a concise method of communicating and documenting judgments regarding the quantity of risk, the quality of risk management, the level of supervisory concern (measured as aggregate risk), and the direction of risk.[22] The three-part supervisory framework (core knowledge, core assessment, and expanded procedures) and the RAS enable the OCC to measure and assess existing and emerging risks in banks, regardless of their size or complexity.

Once these risk assessments have been made, examiners should discuss them with bank management and the board. If a change to the RAS occurs that would alter the bank's supervisory strategy, examiners should formally communicate the rationale for the change to the bank. These communications will help the bank and the OCC reach a common understanding of the risks, focus on the strengths and weaknesses of risk management, and ensure that supervisory objectives are achieved.

Relationship of RAS and Regulatory Ratings

The risk assessment system and the uniform interagency rating systems are distinct yet closely related evaluation methods used during the supervisory process. Both provide information about a bank's

---

[22] A full discussion of the RAS can be found in the "Community Bank Supervision" and "Large Bank Supervision" booklets.

- Overall soundness.
- Financial and operational weaknesses or adverse trends.
- Problems or deteriorating conditions.
- Risk management practices.

Because of these commonalities, the RAS and the rating systems can and do affect one another. For example, examiners may assess credit risk in a bank with weak risk management practices and increasing adverse trends as "moderate and increasing" or "high and increasing." If the component rating for asset quality does not reflect the level of supervisory concern posed by credit risk, the rating should be lowered. When the two methods are used in this manner, they provide an important verification of supervisory findings and planned activities.

The major distinction between the RAS and rating systems is the prospective nature of the RAS. The rating systems primarily provide a point-in-time assessment of an institution's current performance. The RAS reflects both a current (aggregate risk) and a prospective (direction of risk) view of the institution's risk profile.

Supervisory Framework

The OCC's supervisory framework—core knowledge, core assessment, and expanded procedures—guides examiners in determining the bank's risk profile.[23] The supervisory framework enables examiners to tailor examination activities to the level of risk within any given examination area.

Core knowledge provides a foundation for risk assessment by capturing elements of the bank's culture, risk tolerance, products and services, and other internal and external factors. Core knowledge helps the examiner determine when to expand supervisory activities beyond the core assessment.

The core assessment establishes the minimum conclusions examiners must reach to assess risks and assign uniform ratings. Using the core assessment, examiners evaluate the quantity of risk and the quality of risk management separately. They also determine how much supporting detail or work is required in each area by considering the condition of the bank, the nature of risks, the components of risk management, the background and experience of the examination team, and other relevant information.[24]

For areas in which risks are higher, or for complex activities, examiners may use the expanded procedures, which contain additional guidance. Examiners can decide whether to use expanded procedures during examination planning or after reviewing the findings and conclusions of core assessments.

---

[23] Refer to "Philosophy" for definitions of these terms.

[24] A full discussion of the core assessment can be found in the "Community Bank Supervision" and "Large Bank Supervision" booklets.

The Supervisory Process

The OCC fulfills its mission principally through its program to supervise national banks on an ongoing basis. Examining is more than just on-site activities that result in an examination report. It includes discovery of a bank's condition, ensuring correction of significant deficiencies, and monitoring the bank's activities and progress. In large and mid-size banks, examination activities occur throughout the 12-month supervisory cycle. In smaller national bank affiliates, community banks, and federal branches and agencies, there is flexibility in both when and how examination activities are performed during the 12- or 18-month supervisory cycle. Regardless of the size or complexity of the bank, all OCC examination activities depend on careful planning, effective management throughout the supervisory cycle, and clear communication of results to bank management and the board.

Planning

Planning is essential to effective supervision. During planning, examiners develop detailed strategies for providing effective, efficient supervision to each bank or company. Planning requires careful and thoughtful assessment of a bank's current and anticipated risks. In other words, examiners should assess the risks of both existing and new banking activities. New banking activities may be either traditional activities that are new to the bank or activities new to the financial services industry.[25] The supervisory strategy should also incorporate an assessment of the company's merger and acquisition plans and any conditions attached to corporate decisions.

Supervisory Strategy

A completed RAS is the foundation for planning. Conclusions from the RAS are used to develop supervisory strategies. Supervisory strategies outline all planned supervisory activities and help ensure that sufficient resources are available to address bank risks and fulfill statutory requirements. Strategies are dynamic documents that are reviewed and updated frequently based on company, industry, economic, legislative, and regulatory developments. Examiners should discuss strategies with bank management as the plans are made and whenever significantly modified.

Supervisory strategies are unique to each bank or company. Each strategy is based on

- The **core knowledge** of the bank, including its
  - Risk profile.
  - Ratings.
  - Management.
  - Control environment.
  - Audit functions.
  - Market(s).

---

[25] Refer to OCC Bulletin 2004-20, "Risk Management of New, Expanded, or Modified Bank Products and Services."

- Products and activities.
- Information technology support and services.

- OCC supervisory guidance and other factors, including
  - Supervisory history.
  - Core assessment.
  - Other examination guidelines (e.g., expanded procedures in the *Comptroller's Handbook* and the FFIEC *IT Examination Handbook*).
  - Supervisory priorities of the agency that may arise from time to time.
  - Applicable economic conditions.

- Statutory examination requirements.

The portfolio manager or EIC, in collaboration with the supervisory office and specialty examiners, develops the supervisory strategy. The strategy integrates all supervisory activities that will be completed during the supervisory cycle.

The supervisory strategy comprises objectives, activities, and work plans:

- **Objectives** define the goals of supervision for the specific institution or company, based on its risk profile. They are the foundation for all activities and work plans. Well-defined objectives allow supervisory activities to be focused and efficient. They also help OCC managers ensure consistent and appropriate application of supervisory policy and resources. The objectives must be clear, attainable, specific, and action-oriented.

- **Activities** are the means of achieving supervisory objectives. Each activity must be linked to at least one objective. Activities must ensure that the core assessment is performed during the applicable supervisory cycle for safety and soundness and specialty areas. Activities should outline communication plans, including board meetings. The type, depth, and frequency of activities undertaken should correspond to the level of risk in each bank and statutory requirements. However, examiners should employ some periodic baseline transaction testing to validate key control functions and systems, even if those areas are considered low risk.

  When engaging in activities, examiners should not take on burdens and costs that are the bank's responsibility. Once the OCC has identified a problem or deficiency and its potential cause, the bank should use its resources to fully determine the extent of the deficiency. The OCC will review the bank's work and test its reliability. The exception is in problem banks, especially failing banks, banks in which fraudulent activities are suspected, and banks with severe BSA deficiencies. In these situations, examiners will do detailed evaluations of the depth and nature of the problem.

- **Work plans** describe how objectives will be achieved. They outline the scope, timing, and resources needed to meet the supervisory objectives and activities.

Strategies must cover a sufficient period of time to allow for effective planning and scheduling of OCC resources. Specifically,

- For a large or mid-size bank on a 12-month supervisory cycle, the plan must encompass 15 months (five quarters) so that it always covers 12 months when it is next updated.

- For a community bank or a federal branch or agency, the plan must detail fully the examination and periodic monitoring activities during the supervisory cycle.

While OCC examiners follow risk-based strategies for individual banks, they are also guided by a supervisory operating plan for the national banking system. The operating plan, which is revised periodically, conveys the agency's general supervisory concerns.

Examination Planning

Planning extends beyond the development of supervisory strategies. Each supervisory activity must be carefully planned to ensure effective supervision and efficient use of OCC resources. Prior to the start of a supervisory activity, the EIC or designee should

- Review the supervisory strategy and OCC information systems (e.g., SIS-EV, WISDM, Canary, Customer Assistance Group (CAG) complaint reports).
- As appropriate, discuss the bank and associated risks with the portfolio manager/EIC or ADC.
- Contact bank management to discuss the examination scope and objectives and changes in bank operations, controls, and personnel.
- Modify the supervisory strategy, if necessary.
- Prepare a scope memo if the scope of the examination has been expanded.
- Coordinate the examination with other regulatory agencies, as necessary.
- Determine staffing assignments.
- Send a request letter to the bank.
- Perform analysis of any advance information provided by the bank.
- Communicate assignments and other information to examining staff.

Coordination with Other Regulators

Effective planning, especially for large, complex, internationally active and diversified companies, requires adequate and timely communication among supervisory agencies. Depending on the scope of a bank's operations, coordination may include contact with domestic and foreign bank and nonbank regulators.[26] Supervisory personnel should establish and maintain regular communication with designated points of contact at all agencies supervising functional lines of business. These points of contact will assist examiners in the supervision of the consolidated entity by facilitating the exchange of necessary information, the coordination of supervisory activities, and the communication of critical issues.

---

[26] Examiners can find information on coordination with foreign supervisors in PPM 5500-1 (Revised).

In order to determine the overall risk profile of the bank, examiners must consider the risks posed by external market forces and significant lines of business, including those subject to the primary supervision of other regulators. While examiners are not responsible for the ongoing supervision of business lines supervised by other functional regulators, they should obtain information to assess the quantity of risks from those business lines and the risk management systems in place to address those risks.

Section 305 of the Riegle Community Development and Regulatory Improvement Act of 1994 (CDRI), which amended the Federal Deposit Insurance Corporation Improvement Act of 1991 (FDICIA), 12 USC 1820(d), requires each federal banking agency, to the extent practical and consistent with principles of safety and soundness, to

- Coordinate examinations to be conducted by that agency at an insured depository institution and its affiliates.
- Coordinate with the other appropriate federal banking agencies in the conduct of such examinations.
- Work to coordinate examinations with appropriate state bank supervisors.
- Use copies of reports of examination made by any other federal banking agencies or appropriate state bank supervisors to eliminate duplicative requests for information.

However, a federal banking agency can conduct a separate examination of an institution for which it is not the primary regulator in an emergency or under other extraordinary circumstances, or when the agency believes a violation of law may have occurred.

Coordinated interagency examinations are intended to minimize disruptions and burdens associated with the examination process, and to centralize and streamline examinations in multibank organizations. Responsibility for coordinating interagency examinations falls to the OCC office that has supervisory authority for the lead national bank of a multibank holding company, the national bank affiliates of a multibank holding company with a lead state bank, or the lead national bank in a chain banking group.[27]

OCC also shares supervision with other banking regulators on issues related to shared national credits,[28] Interagency Country Exposure Review Committee (ICERC) decisions,[29] and technology service providers (TSPs), including multi-regional data processing servicers (MDPS).[30] When planning supervisory activities, examiners must follow existing written sharing agreements, delegation orders, interagency agreements, internal guidance, and laws governing cooperation and information-sharing with other regulators.

---

[27] Refer to Banking Bulletin 93-38, "Interagency Examination Coordination Guidelines."

[28] The Shared National Credit (SNC) Program is an interagency program designed to provide a review and credit quality assessment of many of the largest and most complex bank credits. Examiners can find more information on the program in PPM 5100-2 (Revised).

[29] The OCC, the FDIC, and the Federal Reserve Board established ICERC to ensure consistent treatment of the transfer risk associated with banks' foreign exposures to both public and private sector entities. Examiners can reference the "Guide to the ICERC Process" for more information.

[30] MDPS examinations are conducted on a joint basis by the federal bank regulatory agencies and are administered by the FFIEC IT Subcommittee. Refer to the "Supervision of Technology Service Providers" booklet of the *FFIEC IT Examination Handbook* for details.

Examining

Examining involves discovering a bank's condition, ensuring the bank corrects significant deficiencies, and monitoring ongoing activities. When assessing the bank's condition, examiners must consider the risk associated with activities performed by the bank and its nonbank subsidiaries and affiliates. Examiners must meet certain minimum objectives during the supervisory cycle, which are defined in the core assessments.[31]

Discovery

Discovery is ongoing and dynamic. Through discovery, examiners gain a fundamental understanding of the condition of the bank, the quality of management, and the effectiveness of risk management systems. Discovery enables examiners to focus on the areas of greatest concern.

In discovery, examiners

- Evaluate the bank's condition.
- Identify significant risks.
- Quantify the risk.
- Evaluate management's and the board's awareness and understanding of significant risks.
- Assess the quality of risk management.
- Perform sufficient testing to verify the integrity of risk management systems (internal and external audits and internal controls).
- Identify unwarranted levels of risk, deficiencies in risk management systems, and the underlying causes of any deficiencies.

A primary objective of discovery is to verify the integrity of risk management systems. The examiner should particularly focus on the evaluation of audit programs and internal control systems.[32] Validation of a bank's audit program in conjunction with its control environment must occur every supervisory cycle, guided by the core assessment.

Examiners use a progressive three-step process to validate the bank's audit program, commencing with a work paper review. If the required internal audit work paper review identifies significant discrepancies or weaknesses in the audit program or the control environment, examiners will expand the examination of those areas and any affected operational or functional business areas. Examiners will use, when appropriate, internal control questionnaires (ICQs) in conjunction with the expanded procedures. After completion of these expanded procedures, if concerns remain about the adequacy of audit and internal

---

[31] The core assessments can be found in the "Large Bank Supervision," the "Community Bank Supervision," and the "Federal Branches and Agencies Supervision" booklets, and the minimum procedures of the *FFIEC BSA/AML Examination Manual.*

[32] For additional information about the process for evaluating internal and external audits and internal controls, refer to the following booklets of the *Comptroller's Handbook*: "Internal and External Audits," "Internal Control," "Large Bank Supervision," and "Community Bank Supervision."

controls, or the integrity of the bank's financial or risk management controls, examiners will further expand the scope of the review by completing verification procedures.[33]

To meet discovery objectives in higher risk areas, examiners use expanded procedures in other booklets of the *Comptroller's Handbook* and the FFIEC *IT Examination Handbook.*

The examiner's evaluations and assessments form the foundation for future supervisory activities. Many of these assessments are captured in the core knowledge database. Bank supervision is an ongoing process that enables examiners to periodically confirm and update their assessments to reflect current or emerging risks. This revalidation is fundamental to effective supervision.

Correction

In the correction process, examiners seek bank management's commitment to correct significant deficiencies and verify that the bank's corrective actions have been successful and timely.

In correction, examiners

- Solicit commitments from management to correct each significant deficiency.
- Review bank-prepared action plans to resolve each significant deficiency, including the appropriateness of the time frames for correction.
- Verify that the bank is executing the action plans.
- Evaluate whether actions the bank has taken or plans to take adequately address the deficiencies.
- Resolve open supervisory issues through informal or formal actions.

Examiners should ensure that bank management's efforts to correct deficiencies address *root causes* rather than symptoms. To do so, examiners may require management to develop new systems or improve the design and implementation of existing systems or processes.

The bank's plans for corrective actions should be formally communicated through action plans. Action plans detail steps or methods management has determined will correct the root causes of deficiencies. Bank management is responsible for developing and executing action plans. Directors are expected to hold management accountable for executing action plans.

Action plans should

- Specify actions to correct deficiencies.
- Address the underlying root causes of significant deficiencies.
- Set realistic time frames for completion.
- Establish benchmarks to measure progress toward completion.
- Identify the bank personnel who will be responsible for correction.

---

[33] ICQs and verification procedures can be found on *Examiner's Library* and the *e files* CDs.

- Detail how the board and management will monitor actions and ensure effective execution of the plan.

The OCC's supervision of deficient areas focuses on verifying execution of the action plan and validating its success. When determining whether to take further action, examiners consider the responsiveness of the bank in recognizing the problem and formulating an effective solution. When the bank is unresponsive or unable to effect resolution, the OCC may take more formal steps to ensure correction.[34]

Monitoring

Ongoing monitoring allows the OCC to respond promptly to risks facing individual banks and the industry as a whole. Monitoring is essential to the supervision of all banks. It allows resources to be redirected to areas of increasing or emerging risk. Monitoring also provides a better focus for onsite examination activities.

In monitoring a bank, examiners

- Identify current and prospective issues that affect the bank's risk profile or overall condition.
- Determine how to focus future supervisory strategies.
- Measure the bank's progress in correcting deficiencies.
- Communicate with management regarding areas of concern, if any.

Examiners must tailor monitoring to each bank or company. When supervising a large bank, for example, examiners primarily monitor the consolidated company, including any potential material risks posed by functionally regulated activities.[35]

Examination Management

To manage an examination effectively, the EIC must provide an organized environment in which supervisory goals and objectives can be achieved within appropriate time frames. The EIC also must ensure that examination controls and procedures provide an orderly way in which to administer and record examination activities.

During the examination, examining staff must inform the EIC of preliminary conclusions, and the EIC must evaluate progress toward completing the supervisory objectives. In some cases, conclusions based on preliminary findings may be sufficient to satisfy examination objectives, thereby allowing resources to be reallocated to other tasks. In other cases, identified issues may require expanding the scope of the examination.

---

[34] See "Enforcement Actions."

[35] Further information on monitoring requirements can be found in the "Large Bank Supervision" and "Community Bank Supervision" booklets.

As representatives of the OCC, the conduct of examiners during an examination must be professional. All members of the examining team will

- Ensure the confidentiality of bank records.
- Conduct meetings and gather information efficiently to minimize disruption of the bank's operations.
- Adhere to schedules for meetings and appointments, including providing updates to bank management during the examination.
- Discuss needs for timely information.
- Give bankers the opportunity to explain the reasons for their actions.
- Be respectful of the opinions of bankers and locally based groups.
- Handle any conflicts in a tactful and professional manner.

Communication

Communication is essential to high-quality bank supervision. The OCC is committed to ongoing, effective communication with the banks that it supervises and with other banking and functional regulators. Maintaining regular communication with designated points of contact at these regulatory agencies facilitates the exchange of critical information, and ensures more effective and efficient supervision.

Communication includes formal and informal conversations and meetings, examination reports, and other written materials. Regardless of form, communications should convey a consistent opinion of the bank's condition. All OCC communications must be professional, objective, clear, and informative. Examiners should have no communications with banks that could be perceived as suggesting that the examination process is in any way influenced by political issues or considerations.[36]

Communication should be ongoing throughout the supervision process and must be tailored to a bank's structure and dynamics. The timing and form of communication depends on the situation being addressed. Examiners should communicate with the bank's management and board as often as the bank's condition and supervisory findings require. Examiners must include detailed plans for communication in the supervisory strategy for the bank or company.

By meeting with management often and directors as needed, examiners can ensure that all current issues are discussed. These discussions, which establish and maintain open lines of communication, are an important source of monitoring information. At entrance and general meetings with bank management before and during examinations, examiners collect information and discuss supervisory issues. When an examination is complete, examiners meet with the board to discuss the results of the examination and other topics. Examiners should document these meetings as appropriate in the OCC's supervisory information systems.

---

[36] Examiners can refer to PPM 1000-11, "Communications with Banks in the Examination Process."

Examiners must clearly and concisely communicate significant weaknesses or unwarranted risks to bank management, allowing management an opportunity to resolve differences, commit to corrective action, or correct the weakness. Examiners should describe the weaknesses, as well as the board's or management's commitment to corrective action, as "Matters Requiring Attention" (MRA) in the ROE or in other periodic written communication.[37]

Entrance Meetings with Management

The EIC will meet with appropriate holding company or bank management at the beginning of an examination to

- Explain the scope of the examination, the role of each examiner, and how the examination team will conduct the examination.
- Confirm the availability of bank personnel.
- Identify communication contacts.
- Answer any questions.

If an examination will be conducted jointly with another regulator, the OCC should invite a representative from that agency to participate in the entrance meeting.

Communications during Examinations

Periodic meetings with bank management are essential during the examination. Discussion of key issues and preliminary findings prevents misunderstanding and allows bank management to provide additional information. Every effort must be made to resolve significant differences concerning material findings, conclusions, or recommendations. In communications with the bank and the OCC supervisory office, examiners must accurately describe bank management's position on any remaining differences. Ongoing communication and discussion ensures that examiners derive conclusions from sound and accurate information.

The EIC will communicate, as necessary, with the appropriate OCC supervisory office regarding examination progress. The EIC should discuss preliminary conclusions, substantive violations, potential "problem bank" situations, possible civil money penalty (CMP) referrals, and any other significant issues. Contact with OCC legal staff, subject matter experts, or specialty examiners may be appropriate for significant supervisory matters.

Exit Meetings with Management

After each significant supervisory activity is completed, the EIC will meet with bank or company management to discuss findings, any significant issues, the areas of greatest risk to the bank, preliminary ratings, and plans for future supervisory activities. The EIC should encourage bankers to respond to OCC concerns, provide clarification, ask about future

---

[37] Refer to appendix I for the definition of and guidance on Matters Requiring Attention.

supervisory plans, and raise any other questions or concerns. At the exit meeting, the examiners will ask for management's commitment to correct weaknesses noted during the supervisory activity and will, when appropriate, offer examples of acceptable solutions to identified problems. In preparing conclusions, examiners will consider the significance and benefit of their recommendations and the potential impact, such as cost, on the bank's operations.

In large or departmentalized banks, examiners may conduct exit meetings with management of specific departments or functions before the final exit meeting. The functional EICs summarize the issues and commitments for corrective actions from these meetings. The bank EIC then discusses them with senior bank management at the final exit meeting.

Before the exit meeting, the EIC should discuss significant findings, including preliminary ratings, with the appropriate OCC supervisory office. This discussion helps ensure that OCC policy is consistently applied and that OCC management supports the conclusions and any corrective action. The EIC and the supervisory office should also decide who will attend the exit meeting on behalf of the OCC, and inquire about the attendance of senior bank managers and others. If the examination was conducted jointly with another regulator, the supervisory office should invite a representative from that agency to participate in the exit meeting.

Examiners must ensure that any significant decisions discussed during the exit meeting are effectively conveyed in the meeting with the board **and** in written correspondence. Examiners should discuss all issues with management before discussing them with the board, unless, in the supervisory office's view, the subject is best approached confidentially with the board.

Written Communication

Written communication of supervisory activities and findings is essential to effective supervision. Examiners should periodically provide written communication to the board highlighting significant issues that arise during the supervisory process. The communication should focus the board's attention on the OCC's major conclusions, including any significant problems. This record, along with other related correspondence, helps establish and support the OCC's supervisory strategy.

Written communication must

- Be consistent with the tone, findings, and conclusions orally communicated to the bank.
- Convey the condition of the bank or, if appropriate, the condition of an operational unit of the bank.
- Be addressed to the appropriate audience based on how the bank or company is structured and managed.
- Discuss any concerns the OCC has about bank risks, deficiencies in risk management, or significant violations.
- Summarize the actions and commitments that the OCC will require of the bank to correct deficiencies and violations.

- Be concise to ensure that the issues are clear.

The OCC must provide a bank's board of directors a report of examination (ROE) at least once each supervisory cycle (12 or 18 months). The ROE conveys the overall condition and risk profile of the bank, and summarizes examination activities and findings during the supervisory cycle. The ROE

- Contains conclusions on assigned ratings and the adequacy of the bank's BSA/AML compliance program;
- Discusses significant deficiencies, violations, and excessive risks; and
- Details corrective action to which the board or management has committed.

Since 1993, the OCC has used the interagency uniform common core ROE format.[38] More recently, the federal banking agencies agreed to a flexible approach in using this format for examination reports.[39]

Examiners may choose to formally communicate the results of activities conducted during the supervisory cycle as they occur. Those results are then also included in the ROE issued at the end of the cycle. However, significant deficiencies and excessive risks must be promptly communicated to the bank whenever they are identified either by sending a written communication to the board or by meeting with the board or management. Written communication is required if there is any significant change in an aggregate risk assessment or any CAMELS/ITC rating. Examiners are not required to use the ROE for interim communication; any appropriate format may be used.

During the course of the supervisory cycle, the supervisory office may receive correspondence and other information from banks. As a matter of policy, examiners will respond to information received from banks within 30 days of receipt and document the correspondence in the OCC's supervisory information systems.

Meetings with Directors

The OCC maintains communication with boards of directors throughout the supervisory cycle to discuss OCC examination results and other matters of mutual interest, including current industry issues, emerging industry risks, and legislative issues. The EIC will meet with the board of directors or an authorized committee that includes outside directors after the board or committee has reviewed the report of examination findings. If necessary, the OCC will use board meetings to discuss how the board should respond to supervisory concerns and issues.

Large and mid-size banks. The OCC will conduct a board meeting at least once during the 12-month supervisory cycle for the lead national bank. More frequent meetings should be conducted when justified by the bank's condition or special supervisory needs. When

---

[38] See Examining Bulletin 93-7, "Interagency Common Core Report of Examination."
[39] Refer to appendix I, "ROE Content, Structure, and Review Requirements."

meetings are routinely conducted with board committees, examiners are also encouraged to meet periodically with the full board to confirm findings and facilitate effective communication. Examiners should conduct board meetings with affiliated national banks that are not lead banks only when significant supervisory concerns exist or when meetings will enhance overall supervision. Senior management of the appropriate OCC supervisory office should attend and participate in board meetings with large and mid-size banks.

Community banks and federal branches and agencies. The OCC will conduct a board meeting at least once during each supervisory cycle (12 or 18 months), normally at the conclusion of the cycle. Sometimes, an exit meeting with management can be combined with the board meeting (e.g., when examiners have no significant concerns and when travel time and costs favor it). Meetings with the board should be more frequent if examiners need to discuss supervisory concerns or other items of significance. The EIC and the ADC or a representative from the supervisory office should attend the board meeting. If the ADC does not attend a board meeting where examination results are discussed, he or she may attend an examination exit meeting with board members attending or a regularly scheduled board meeting at any time during the supervisory cycle.

Before a board meeting, the EIC should discuss the agenda with the supervisory office to ensure that the meeting emphasizes the proper topics. The EIC and the supervisory office should also discuss who will attend the board meeting on behalf of the OCC and the role of each attendee. If the examination was conducted jointly with another regulator, the supervisory office or EIC should invite a representative from that agency to participate in the board meeting.

The EIC should also discuss with senior bank management who will attend the board meeting on behalf of the bank and determine whether any guests of the board will attend. In certain serious situations, specific board members, management officials, or guests of board members should not attend the board meeting (or certain parts of it). For example, when discussing specific insider issues, the insider involved should normally be excused from that discussion.

Documentation

Examiners must document their decisions and conclusions regarding the national banks under their supervision. Supervisory offices must also document actions they take with respect to individual national banks. These actions include, but are not limited to, decisions regarding enforcement actions, corporate applications, and other formal communications.

Documentation includes correspondence, reports of examination, work papers, and records of key meetings. Work papers may be in electronic or paper form and in most cases need not include all of the information reviewed during a supervisory activity. Generally, only those documents necessary to support the scope of the supervisory activity, significant conclusions, ratings changes, or changes in the risk profile should be generated and retained as work papers.[40] Examiners should be guided by OCC's information security policies when handling and storing sensitive bank examination work papers in either electronic or paper form.

Examiners must document **all** violations of laws and regulations in work papers and the OCC's supervisory information systems. Significant violations must also be discussed in the report of examination. Technical violations that are not attributable to a pattern of negligent behavior or poor operating policies or procedures, and violations that have been or soon will be corrected because of prompt action by bank personnel, generally should not be discussed in the examination report. These violations should be provided to bank management in a list.

OCC's Supervisory Information Systems

Examiners record and communicate narrative and statistical information on institutions of supervisory interest to the OCC through the agency's supervisory information systems.[41] These institutions include banks, holding companies and affiliates, federal branches and agencies of foreign banks, and independent technology service providers.

The recorded information will reflect the current condition, supervisory strategy, and supervisory concerns for each bank. It also documents follow-up actions, board meeting discussions, commitments to corrective action, progress in correcting identified problems, and significant events. Using these electronic records, OCC senior management can review the condition of individual banks and groups of banks. Other federal banking regulators also have access to the information, as appropriate, through various formats.

Many electronic files are official records of the OCC and may be discoverable items in litigation. When writing electronic comments, examiners must be succinct, clear, and professional, avoiding any informality that might be misunderstood or misused.

The EIC, portfolio manager, and the supervisory office are responsible for ensuring that the electronic files for their assigned institutions are accurate and up-to-date. For individual community banks and federal branches and agencies, examiners should enter information under the appropriate charter number. For large banks, examiners should record information as follows:

- Comments pertaining to or affecting the entire company should be recorded in the electronic file under the consolidated company.

- Comments particular to a bank should be recorded in the electronic file under that bank.

---

[40] For example, examiners should clearly document their completion of the minimum BSA/AML examination procedures consistent with OCC policy. For information regarding the OCC's policy and standards for establishing and maintaining work papers, see PPM 5400-8 (Revised), "Supervision Work Papers."
[41] OCC policy guidance on updating and maintaining supervisory information systems is contained in the WISDM User's Guide; PPM 5000-35, "Examiner View"; and the SIS-Examiner View Help system.

Other Supervisory Considerations

Conditions Imposed in Writing

The OCC may impose enforceable conditions in connection with the approval of any application or other request by a bank to

- Protect the safety and soundness of the bank;
- Prevent conflicts of interest;
- Ensure that the bank provides customer protections;
- Ensure that the approval is consistent with laws and regulations; or
- Provide for other supervisory or policy considerations.

These conditions are "conditions imposed in writing" within the meaning of 12 USC 1818. They frequently are used by the OCC in approvals of corporate applications and interpretive letter opinions on requests to engage in permissible activities. These conditions remain in effect until the OCC removes them.

Examiners should ensure that supervisory strategies include periodic assessments of the bank's ongoing compliance with any approval conditions. If a bank is found in violation, a Matter Requiring Attention should be cited in the ROE and documented in the OCC's supervisory information systems.

Enforcement Actions

Enforcement action is a collective term that refers to a range of supervisory actions used to correct problems, concerns, weaknesses, or deficiencies noted in a national bank. Enforcement action can also be based upon a bank's violation of laws, rules, regulations, or conditions imposed in writing. These actions range from informal written commitments to formal enforcement actions, prompt corrective action (PCA) directives, and safety and soundness orders. The OCC uses formal or informal enforcement actions to carry out its supervisory responsibilities. Examiners recommend these actions when they identify safety and soundness or compliance problems in a national bank.

The ROE is not an enforcement action, but an effective ROE can serve the same purpose as an informal enforcement action by setting out a blueprint for addressing problems and preventing them from worsening. The ROE should not detail every remedial measure necessary to address identified problems, but it should give clear guidance to the bank on what is expected. The actions a bank takes or agrees to take to correct identified problems are important factors in determining whether the OCC will take enforcement action and the severity of that action. When the OCC takes enforcement action, the ROE must support the type of action taken.

Informal enforcement actions give a bank more explicit guidance and direction than an ROE. Informal actions require a written commitment from the bank's board members. These actions serve as evidence of the board's commitment to correct identified problems before they affect the bank's condition. Informal enforcement actions include commitment letters, memoranda of understanding, and approved safety and soundness plans.

Formal enforcement actions are statutorily authorized or mandated, are generally more severe than informal actions, and are disclosed to the public. They are used when informal actions are inadequate or ineffective in influencing bank management and board members to correct identified problems and concerns in the bank's operations. Formal enforcement actions include formal written agreements, consent orders, cease and desist orders, temporary cease and desist orders, capital directives, prompt corrective action (PCA) directives, and safety and soundness orders. They also include decisions to place a bank into conservatorship or receivership.

The recommendation for a specific enforcement action should be tailored to the bank and designed to correct identified deficiencies and return the bank to a safe and sound condition. Once an enforcement action is in place, examiners must periodically assess the bank's compliance, generally at least every six months. Written feedback must be provided to bank management and the board, and the assessment should be documented in the OCC's supervisory information systems. PPM 5310-3 (Revised) and its Supplement 1 detail the OCC's enforcement action policy. (This PPM is available to banks as an attachment to OCC Bulletins 2002-38 and 2004-51.) OCC Bulletin 2007-36 provides guidance on enforcement of BSA/AML requirements.

Civil Money Penalties

Civil money penalties (CMPs), which require monetary payments, penalize directors or other persons participating in the affairs of the bank for violations of laws, regulations, orders, conditions imposed in writing, written agreements, unsafe or unsound practices, and breaches of fiduciary duty. CMPs may be used alone or in combination with informal or formal enforcement actions.

Although the OCC may impose CMPs on banks, they are assessed principally against individuals. PPM 5000-7 (Revised) sets forth the OCC's policy on assessment of CMPs, and PPM 5000-27 (Revised) separately details the OCC's policy on assessment of CMPs against national banks for filing delinquent or inaccurate call reports. (PPM 5000-7 is attached to Banking Circular 273, and PPM 5000-27 is attached to Banking Circular 270.) In addition, the OCC must assess CMPs if it finds that a national bank has engaged in a pattern or practice of violations of certain requirements under the Flood Disaster Protection Act (42 USC 4012a(f)).

Examiners should propose CMPs for serious misconduct, including misconduct that is reckless, flagrant, willful, or knowing and that, because of its frequency or recurring nature, shows a general disregard for the law. Added consideration should be given to violations that occurred or continued in direct contravention of the bank's policy guidelines, correspondence from the regulator, or audit reports.

After reviewing the facts and deciding to recommend a CMP, the examiner should immediately contact the appropriate supervisory office and legal counsel for advice on proper documentation and any other assistance. The examiner should submit a CMP referral to the supervisory office within 30 days of the close of the examination. The referral should include a memorandum containing the EIC's recommendations, a completed CMP matrix, and necessary supporting documentation.

In certain cases, the issuance of a reprimand or a supervisory letter may be more appropriate than the assessment of a CMP. A reprimand is a strongly worded document used in lieu of a CMP when, for example, the CMP would be too small to justify spending agency resources required or when the individual or institution has recognized the supervisory problem and taken steps to correct it. A supervisory letter is generally used to call attention to a supervisory problem that is not severe enough to warrant a CMP.

Examiners should notify management and the board at the exit meeting and in the ROE whenever they are recommending CMPs or a reprimand. Examiners should refer management to PPM 5000-7 (Revised) and discuss the policy. This discussion should include descriptions of the CMP process and the criteria the OCC uses to decide whether to assess a penalty and to set the amount. The examiner should not discuss or speculate on the amount of any penalty, but may refer the board and management to the CMP matrix. Examiners must document CMP referrals and discussions of referrals with bank management in the OCC's supervisory information systems.

Suspected Criminal Violations

Banks are required by 12 CFR 21.11(c) to report violations of federal criminal law to the Financial Crimes Enforcement Network (FinCEN) on a Suspicious Activity Report (SAR). This form must be filed when known or suspected criminal violations involve actual or potential loss of any amount when insider abuse is involved, $5,000 or more when a suspect can be identified, $25,000 or more regardless of a potential suspect, or $5,000 or more when potential money laundering or violations of the Bank Secrecy Act are involved.

If examiners discover a suspected criminal violation subject to the reporting guidelines, they should instruct bank management to file a SAR. However, for violations involving a significant loss to the bank, insider abuse, or the Federal Election Campaign Act of 1971,[42] examiners must consult OCC legal counsel prior to notifying the bank. OCC personnel are forbidden from threatening to report suspected criminal violations to the United States Attorney, threatening criminal prosecution, or making offers or promises of immunity under any circumstances. Examiners should not make statements regarding the probability of indictment, conviction, or related matters. In certain cases, the OCC may issue an order of removal or prohibition or require restitution when law enforcement agencies decline to prosecute a bank insider for a criminal act or significant wrongdoing.[43]

---

[42] Refer to OCC Bulletin 2007-31, "Prohibition on Political Contributions by National Banks."
[43] Examiners should see PPM 5310-8 (Revised), "Fast Track Enforcement Program."

Information Received from an Outside Source

When examiners are contacted by an outside source possessing information about alleged misconduct by a bank, its employees, its officers, or its directors, they are occasionally asked to protect the informant's identity. Any request to protect an informant's identity will be evaluated on a case-by-case basis, in consultation with legal counsel.

If possible, the examiner should advise the informant before receiving the information that

- The OCC will try to comply with the request for confidentiality but does not guarantee that it will be able to do so.

- Bank personnel may deduce the informant's identity as a result of any inquiry.

- The OCC may refer the information to another agency, such as the Department of Justice, which may request the informant's identity to continue or complete an investigation.

- The OCC will disclose the informant's identity to another agency only if it agrees to abide by the OCC's promise of confidentiality.

- If the information becomes the basis for criminal prosecution, the court may order disclosure of the informant's identity to the defendant.

- The prosecutor may refuse to identify the informant, but in response the court would probably dismiss the indictment or information.

The examiner should ask the informant for permission to disclose his or her identity to another agency, if required. The informant should report the information only to the EIC of the bank. The EIC should investigate the situation while guarding the informant's identity.

The EIC should not reveal an informant's identity to bank representatives, nor should the EIC discuss the informant's identity with others, except as necessary to perform their official duties. The EIC should explain the OCC's policy of confidentiality to persons outside the agency who request the informant's identity, and should refer all questions to OCC legal counsel.

Appeals Process

The OCC desires consistent and equitable supervision and seeks to resolve disputes that arise during the supervisory process fairly and expeditiously in an informal, professional manner. When disputes can not be resolved informally, a national bank may ask its supervisory office to review the disputed matter or appeal the matter to the OCC Ombudsman.

The OCC Ombudsman is independent of the bank supervision function and reports directly to the Comptroller of the Currency. With the prior consent of the Comptroller, the Ombudsman may stay any appealable agency decision or action during the resolution of the appealable matter.[44] The Ombudsman may also identify and report weaknesses in OCC policy to the Comptroller, and may recommend policy changes.

Customer Assistance Group

The mission of OCC's Customer Assistance Group (CAG), a unit within the Ombudsman's office, is to provide an avenue for customers of national banks and their operating subsidiaries to pursue questions or complaints. The CAG answers questions, provides advice, investigates complaints, and refers customers to the appropriate regulator when the complaint is not about a national bank.

The CAG plays an integral role in assisting OCC bank supervision in assessing compliance and reputation risks within the national banking system. Through the use of Web-based applications such as the CAGWizard, examiners have nearly real-time access to the CAG Complaint Data Base, which contains multiple tools to search out trends by bank or by product. In addition, CAG analysts review complaint volumes, trends, and issues on an ongoing basis and incorporate findings into their analyses. CAG senior management regularly meets with bank executive management to discuss areas of potential risks and opportunities to enhance the bank's quality of customer service.

Quality Management

The bank supervision quality management (QM) programs are designed to ensure that the agency achieves its objectives for bank supervision, as defined in the "Large Bank Supervision" and "Community Bank Supervision" booklets and other related guidance. QM programs typically consist of pre-delivery quality controls, post-delivery quality assurance activities, and management practices intended to promote continuous business process improvement. Separate QM programs have been designed by the Large Bank Supervision and Mid-size/Community Bank Supervision departments to support the policy frameworks established by these two booklets.

All Deputy Comptrollers with supervisory responsibilities certify annually to their Senior Deputy Comptroller that banks in their portfolio are being effectively supervised and that their bank supervision processes are operating in conformance with OCC policy. These certifications highlight systemic examination process concerns identified within their units, as well as innovative bank supervisory practices noted during the conduct of their ongoing quality management activities. Requests for certifications are typically made in June of each year and are due by the end of July.

These certifications are an integral part of the process through which the OCC complies with the Federal Managers Financial Integrity Act (FMFIA). FMFIA and the Government

---

[44] For additional guidance on the appeals process and the definition of an appealable decision or action, refer to OCC Bulletin 2002-9, "National Bank Appeals Process." Examiners may also refer to PPM 1000-9 (Revised), "Administering Appeals from National Banks."

Performance and Results Act (GPRA, commonly known as the "Results Act") set standards for accountability in government.

Enterprise Governance, a unit which reports to the Comptroller through his Chief of Staff, is responsible for testing the integrity of each department's quality management program.

Appendixes

Appendix A: CAMELS Rating System

The Uniform Financial Institutions Rating System (UFIRS) was adopted by the Federal Financial Institutions Examination Council (FFIEC) in 1979 and revised in 1996. The rating system is commonly referred to as the CAMELS rating system because it assesses six components of a bank's performance: Capital adequacy, Asset quality, Management, Earnings, Liquidity, and Sensitivity to market risk.

Introduction

The UFIRS takes into consideration certain financial, managerial, and compliance factors that are common to all institutions. Under this system, the supervisory agencies endeavor to ensure that all financial institutions are evaluated in a comprehensive and uniform manner, and that supervisory attention is appropriately focused on the financial institutions exhibiting financial and operational weaknesses or adverse trends.

The UFIRS also serves as a useful vehicle for identifying problem or deteriorating financial institutions, as well as for categorizing institutions with deficiencies in particular component areas. Further, the rating system assists Congress in following safety and soundness trends and in assessing the aggregate strength and soundness of the financial industry. As such, the UFIRS assists the agencies in fulfilling their collective mission of maintaining stability and public confidence in the nation's financial system.

The OCC considers Bank Secrecy Act/anti-money laundering (BSA/AML) examination findings in a safety and soundness context when assigning the management component rating. Serious deficiencies in a bank's BSA/AML compliance create a presumption that the management rating will be adversely affected because risk management practices are less than satisfactory. Examiners should document application of this approach in their written comments in the OCC's supervisory information systems, and in supervisory communications, when appropriate. (Updated 9/28/2012)

Overview[45]

Under the UFIRS, each financial institution is assigned a composite rating based on an evaluation and rating of six essential components of an institution's financial condition and operations. These component factors address the adequacy of capital, the quality of assets, the capability of management, the quality and level of earnings, the adequacy of liquidity, and the sensitivity to market risk. Evaluations of the components take into consideration the institution's size and sophistication, the nature and complexity of its activities, and its risk profile.

---

[45] Excerpts taken from Federal Register, Volume 61, No. 245, December 19, 1996, pages 67021-67029, Uniform Financial Institutions Rating System.

Composite and component ratings are assigned based on a 1 to 5 numerical scale. A 1 is the highest rating, and indicates strongest performance and risk management practices, and least degree of supervisory concern, while a 5 is the lowest rating, and indicates weakest performance, inadequate risk management practices and, therefore, the highest degree of supervisory concern.

The composite rating generally bears a close relationship to the component ratings assigned. However, the composite rating is not derived by computing an arithmetic average of the component ratings. Each component rating is based on a qualitative analysis of the factors comprising that component and its interrelationship with the other components. When assigning a composite rating, some components may be given more weight than others depending on the situation at the institution. In general, assignment of a composite rating may incorporate any factor that bears significantly on the overall condition and soundness of the financial institution. Assigned composite and component ratings are disclosed to the institution's board of directors and senior management.

The ability of management to respond to changing circumstances and to address the risks that may arise from changing business conditions, or the initiation of new activities or products, is an important factor in evaluating a financial institution's overall risk profile and the level of supervisory attention warranted. For this reason, the management component is given special consideration when assigning a composite rating.

The ability of management to identify, measure, monitor, and control the risks of its operations is also taken into account when assigning each component rating. It is recognized, however, that appropriate management practices vary considerably among financial institutions, depending on their size, complexity, and risk profile. For less complex institutions engaged solely in traditional banking activities and whose directors and senior managers, in their respective roles, are actively involved in the oversight and management of day-to-day operations, relatively basic management systems and controls may be adequate. At more complex institutions, on the other hand, detailed and formal management systems and controls are needed to address their broader range of financial activities and to provide senior managers and directors, in their respective roles, with the information they need to monitor and direct day-to-day activities. All institutions are expected to properly manage their risks. For less complex institutions engaging in less sophisticated risk taking activities, detailed or highly formalized management systems and controls are not required to receive strong or satisfactory component or composite ratings.

Foreign branch and specialty examination findings and the ratings assigned to those areas are taken into consideration, as appropriate, when assigning component and composite ratings under UFIRS. The specialty examination areas include: compliance, community reinvestment, government security dealers, information technology, municipal security dealers, transfer agent, and asset management (trust).

Composite Ratings

Composite ratings are based on a careful evaluation of an institution's managerial, operational, financial, and compliance performance. The six key components used to assess an institution's financial condition and operations are: capital adequacy, asset quality, management capability, earnings quantity and quality, the adequacy of liquidity, and sensitivity to market risk. The rating scale ranges from 1 to 5, with a rating of 1 indicating: the strongest performance and risk management practices relative to the institution's size, complexity, and risk profile; and the level of least supervisory concern. A 5 rating indicates: the most critically deficient level of performance; inadequate risk management practices relative to the institution's size, complexity, and risk profile; and the greatest supervisory concern. The composite ratings are defined as follows:

Composite 1

Financial institutions in this group are sound in every respect and generally have components rated 1 or 2. Any weaknesses are minor and can be handled in a routine manner by the board of directors and management. These financial institutions are the most capable of withstanding the vagaries of business conditions and are resistant to outside influences such as economic instability in their trade area.

These financial institutions are in substantial compliance with laws and regulations. As a result, these financial institutions exhibit the strongest performance and risk management practices relative to the institution's size, complexity, and risk profile, and give no cause for supervisory concern.

Composite 2

Financial institutions in this group are fundamentally sound. For a financial institution to receive this rating, generally no component rating should be more severe than 3. Only moderate weaknesses are present and are well within the board of directors' and management's capabilities and willingness to correct. These financial institutions are stable and are capable of withstanding business fluctuations. These financial institutions are in substantial compliance with laws and regulations. Overall risk management practices are satisfactory relative to the institution's size, complexity, and risk profile. There are no material supervisory concerns and, as a result, the supervisory response is informal and limited.

Composite 3

Financial institutions in this group exhibit some degree of supervisory concern in one or more of the component areas. These financial institutions exhibit a combination of weaknesses that may range from moderate to severe; however, the magnitude of the deficiencies generally will not cause a component to be rated more severely than 4. Management may lack the ability or willingness to effectively address weaknesses within appropriate time frames. Financial institutions in this group generally are less capable of withstanding business fluctuations and are more vulnerable to outside influences than those institutions rated a composite 1 or 2. Additionally, these financial institutions may be in significant noncompliance with laws and regulations. Risk management practices may be less than satisfactory relative to the institution's size, complexity, and risk profile. These financial institutions require more than normal supervision, which may include formal or informal enforcement actions. Failure appears unlikely, however, given the overall strength and financial capacity of these institutions.

Composite 4

Financial institutions in this group generally exhibit unsafe and unsound practices or conditions. There are serious financial or managerial deficiencies that result in unsatisfactory performance. The problems range from severe to critically deficient. The weaknesses and problems are not being satisfactorily addressed or resolved by the board of directors and management. Financial institutions in this group generally are not capable of withstanding business fluctuations. There may be significant noncompliance with laws and regulations. Risk management practices are generally unacceptable relative to the institution's size, complexity, and risk profile. Close supervisory attention is required, which means, in most cases, formal enforcement action is necessary to address the problems. Institutions in this group pose a risk to the deposit insurance fund. Failure is a distinct possibility if the problems and weaknesses are not satisfactorily addressed and resolved.

Composite 5

Financial institutions in this group exhibit extremely unsafe and unsound practices or conditions; exhibit a critically deficient performance; often demonstrate inadequate risk management practices relative to the institution's size, complexity, and risk profile; and are of the greatest supervisory concern. The volume and severity of problems are beyond management's ability or willingness to control or correct. Immediate outside financial or other assistance is needed in order for the financial institution to be viable. Ongoing supervisory attention is necessary. Institutions in this group pose a significant risk to the deposit insurance fund and failure is highly probable.

Component Ratings

Each of the component rating descriptions is divided into three sections: an introductory paragraph; a list of the principal evaluation factors that relate to that component; and a brief description of each numerical rating for that component. Some of the evaluation factors are reiterated under one or more of the other components to reinforce the interrelationship between components. The listing of evaluation factors for each component rating is in no particular order of importance.

Capital Adequacy

A financial institution is expected to maintain capital commensurate with the nature and extent of risks to the institution and the ability of management to identify, measure, monitor, and control these risks. The effect of credit, market, and other risks on the institution's financial condition should be considered when evaluating the adequacy of capital. The types and quantity of risk inherent in an institution's activities will determine the extent to which it may be necessary to maintain capital at levels above required regulatory minimums to properly reflect the potentially adverse consequences that these risks may have on the institution's capital.

The capital adequacy of an institution is rated based upon, but not limited to, an assessment of the following evaluation factors:

- The level and quality of capital and the overall financial condition of the institution.
- The ability of management to address emerging needs for additional capital.
- The nature, trend, and volume of problem assets, and the adequacy of allowances for loan and lease losses and other valuation reserves.
- Balance sheet composition, including the nature and amount of intangible assets, market risk, concentration risk, and risks associated with nontraditional activities.
- Risk exposure represented by off-balance sheet activities.
- The quality and strength of earnings, and the reasonableness of dividends.
- Prospects and plans for growth, as well as past experience in managing growth.
- Access to capital markets and other sources of capital, including support provided by a parent holding company.

Capital Ratings

1 A rating of 1 indicates a strong capital level relative to the institution's risk profile.

2 A rating of 2 indicates a satisfactory capital level relative to the financial institution's risk profile.

3 A rating of 3 indicates a less than satisfactory level of capital that does not fully support the institution's risk profile. The rating indicates a need for improvement, even if the institution's capital level exceeds minimum regulatory and statutory requirements.

4 A rating of 4 indicates a deficient level of capital. In light of the institution's risk profile, viability of the institution may be threatened. Assistance from shareholders or other external sources of financial support may be required.

5 A rating of 5 indicates a critically deficient level of capital such that the institution's viability is threatened. Immediate assistance from shareholders or other external sources of financial support is required.

Asset Quality

The asset quality rating reflects the quantity of existing and potential credit risk associated with the loan and investment portfolios, other real estate owned, and other assets, as well as off-balance sheet transactions. The ability of management to identify, measure, monitor, and control credit risk is also reflected here. The evaluation of asset quality should consider the adequacy of the allowance for loan and lease losses and weigh the exposure to counterparty, issuer, or borrower default under actual or implied contractual agreements. All other risks that may affect the value or marketability of an institution's assets, including, but not limited to, operating, market, reputation, strategic, or compliance risks, should also be considered.

The asset quality of a financial institution is rated based upon, but not limited to, an assessment of the following evaluation factors:

- The adequacy of underwriting standards, soundness of credit administration practices, and appropriateness of risk identification practices.
- The level, distribution, severity, and trend of problem, classified, nonaccrual, restructured, delinquent, and nonperforming assets for both on- and off-balance sheet transactions.
- The adequacy of the allowance for loan and lease losses and other asset valuation reserves.
- The credit risk arising from or reduced by off-balance sheet transactions, such as unfunded commitments, credit derivatives, commercial and standby letters of credit, and lines of credit.
- The diversification and quality of the loan and investment portfolios.
- The extent of securities underwriting activities and exposure to counterparties in trading activities.
- The existence of asset concentrations.
- The adequacy of loan and investment policies, procedures, and practices.
- The ability of management to properly administer its assets, including the timely identification and collection of problem assets.
- The adequacy of internal controls and management information systems.
- The volume and nature of credit documentation exceptions.

Asset Quality Ratings

1   A rating of 1 indicates strong asset quality and credit administration practices. Identified weaknesses are minor in nature and risk exposure is modest in relation to capital protection and management's abilities. Asset quality in such institutions is of minimal supervisory concern.

2   A rating of 2 indicates satisfactory asset quality and credit administration practices. The level and severity of classifications and other weaknesses warrant a limited level of supervisory attention. Risk exposure is commensurate with capital protection and management's abilities.

3   A rating of 3 is assigned when asset quality or credit administration practices are less than satisfactory. Trends may be stable or indicate deterioration in asset quality or an increase in risk exposure. The level and severity of classified assets, other weaknesses, and risks require an elevated level of supervisory concern. There is generally a need to improve credit administration and risk management practices.

4 A rating of 4 is assigned to financial institutions with deficient asset quality or credit administration practices. The levels of risk and problem assets are significant, and inadequately controlled, and they subject the financial institution to potential losses that, if left unchecked, may threaten its viability.

5 A rating of 5 represents critically deficient asset quality or credit administration practices that present an imminent threat to the institution's viability.

Management

The capability of the board of directors and management, in their respective roles, to identify, measure, monitor, and control the risks of an institution's activities and to ensure that a financial institution's safe, sound, and efficient operation in compliance with applicable laws and regulations is reflected in this rating. Generally, directors need not be actively involved in day-to-day operations; however, they must provide clear guidance regarding acceptable risk exposure levels and ensure that appropriate policies, procedures, and practices have been established. Senior management is responsible for developing and implementing policies, procedures, and practices that translate the board's goals, objectives, and risk limits into prudent operating standards.

Depending on the nature and scope of an institution's activities, management practices may need to address some or all of the following risks: credit, market, operating or transaction, reputation, strategic, compliance, legal, liquidity, and other risks. Sound management practices are demonstrated by: active oversight by the board of directors and management; competent personnel; adequate policies, processes, and controls taking into consideration the size and sophistication of the institution; maintenance of an appropriate audit program and internal control environment; and effective risk monitoring and management information systems. This rating should reflect the board's and management's ability as it applies to all aspects of banking operations as well as other financial service activities in which the institution is involved.

The capability and performance of management and the board of directors is rated based upon, but not limited to, an assessment of the following evaluation factors:

- The level and quality of oversight and support of all institution activities by the board of directors and management.
- The ability of the board of directors and management, in their respective roles, to plan for, and respond to, risks that may arise from changing business conditions or the initiation of new activities or products.
- The adequacy of, and conformance with, appropriate internal policies and controls addressing the operations and risks of significant activities.
- The accuracy, timeliness, and effectiveness of management information and risk monitoring systems appropriate for the institution's size, complexity, and risk profile.

The adequacy of audits and internal controls to: promote effective operations and reliable financial and regulatory reporting; safeguard assets; and ensure compliance with laws, regulations, and internal policies.

- Compliance with laws and regulations.
- Responsiveness to recommendations from auditors and supervisory authorities.
- Management depth and succession.
- The extent that the board of directors and management is affected by, or susceptible to, dominant influence or concentration of authority.
- Reasonableness of compensation policies and avoidance of self-dealing.
- Demonstrated willingness to serve the legitimate banking needs of the community.
- The overall performance of the institution and its risk profile.

Management Ratings

1   A rating of 1 indicates strong performance by management and the board of directors and strong risk management practices relative to the institution's size, complexity, and risk profile. All significant risks are consistently and effectively identified, measured, monitored, and controlled. Management and the board have demonstrated the ability to promptly and successfully address existing and potential problems and risks.

2   A rating of 2 indicates satisfactory management and board performance and risk management practices relative to the institution's size, complexity, and risk profile. Minor weaknesses may exist, but are not material to the safety and soundness of the institution and are being addressed. In general, significant risks and problems are effectively identified, measured, monitored, and controlled.

3   A rating of 3 indicates management and board performance that need improvement or risk management practices that are less than satisfactory given the nature of the institution's activities. The capabilities of management or the board of directors may be insufficient for the type, size, or condition of the institution. Problems and significant risks may be inadequately identified, measured, monitored, or controlled.

4   A rating of 4 indicates deficient management and board performance or risk management practices that are inadequate considering the nature of an institution's activities. The level of problems and risk exposure is excessive. Problems and significant risks are inadequately identified, measured, monitored, or controlled and require immediate action by the board and management to preserve the soundness of the institution. Replacing or strengthening management or the board may be necessary.

5   A rating of 5 indicates critically deficient management and board performance or risk management practices. Management and the board of directors have not demonstrated the ability to correct problems and implement appropriate risk management practices. Problems and significant risks are inadequately identified, measured, monitored, or controlled and now threaten the continued viability of the institution. Replacing or strengthening management or the board of directors is necessary.

Earnings

This rating reflects not only the quantity and trend of earnings, but also factors that may affect the sustainability or quality of earnings. The quantity as well as the quality of earnings can be affected by excessive or inadequately managed credit risk that may result in loan losses and require additions to the allowance for loan and lease losses, or by high levels of market risk that may unduly expose an institution's earnings to volatility in interest rates. The quality of earnings may also be diminished by undue reliance on extraordinary gains, nonrecurring events, or favorable tax effects. Future earnings may be adversely affected by an inability to forecast or control funding and operating expenses, improperly executed or ill-advised business strategies, or poorly managed or uncontrolled exposure to other risks.

The rating of an institution's earnings is based upon, but not limited to, an assessment of the following evaluation factors:

- The level of earnings, including trends and stability.
- The ability to provide for adequate capital through retained earnings.
- The quality and sources of earnings.
- The level of expenses in relation to operations.
- The adequacy of the budgeting systems, forecasting processes, and management information systems in general.
- The adequacy of provisions to maintain the allowance for loan and lease losses and other valuation allowance accounts.
- The earnings exposure to market risk, such as interest rate, foreign exchange, and price risks.

Earnings Ratings

1 A rating of 1 indicates earnings that are strong. Earnings are more than sufficient to support operations and maintain adequate capital and allowance levels after consideration is given to asset quality, growth, and other factors affecting the quality, quantity, and trend of earnings.

2 A rating of 2 indicates earnings that are satisfactory. Earnings are sufficient to support operations and maintain adequate capital and allowance levels after consideration is given to asset quality, growth, and other factors affecting the quality, quantity, and trend of earnings. Earnings that are relatively static, or even experiencing a slight decline, may receive a 2 rating provided the institution's level of earnings is adequate in view of the assessment factors listed above.

3 A rating of 3 indicates earnings that need to be improved. Earnings may not fully support operations and provide for the accretion of capital and allowance levels in relation to the institution's overall condition, growth, and other factors affecting the quality, quantity, and trend of earnings.

4 A rating of 4 indicates earnings that are deficient. Earnings are insufficient to support operations and maintain appropriate capital and allowance levels. Institutions so rated may be characterized by erratic fluctuations in net income or net interest margin, the development of significant negative trends, nominal or unsustainable earnings, intermittent losses, or a substantive drop in earnings from the previous years.

5 A rating of 5 indicates earnings that are critically deficient. A financial institution with earnings rated 5 is experiencing losses that represent a distinct threat to its viability through the erosion of capital.

Liquidity

In evaluating the adequacy of a financial institution's liquidity position, consideration should be given to the current level and prospective sources of liquidity compared to funding needs, as well as to the adequacy of funds management practices relative to the institution's size, complexity, and risk profile. In general, funds management practices should ensure that an institution is able to maintain a level of liquidity sufficient to meet its financial obligations in a timely manner and to fulfill the legitimate banking needs of its community. Practices should reflect the ability of the institution to manage unplanned changes in funding sources, as well as react to changes in market conditions that affect the ability to quickly liquidate assets with minimal loss. In addition, funds management practices should ensure that liquidity is not maintained at a high cost, or through undue reliance on funding sources that may not be available in times of financial stress or adverse changes in market conditions.

Liquidity is rated based upon, but not limited to, an assessment of the following evaluation factors:

The adequacy of liquidity sources to meet present and future needs and the ability of the institution to meet liquidity needs without adversely affecting its operations or condition.

- The availability of assets readily convertible to cash without undue loss.
- Access to money markets and other sources of funding.
- The level of diversification of funding sources, both on- and off-balance sheet.
- The degree of reliance on short-term, volatile sources of funds, including borrowings and brokered deposits, to fund longer term assets.
- The trend and stability of deposits.
- The ability to securitize and sell certain pools of assets.
- The capability of management to properly identify, measure, monitor, and control the institution's liquidity position, including the effectiveness of funds management strategies, liquidity policies, management information systems, and contingency funding plans.

Liquidity Ratings

1   A rating of 1 indicates strong liquidity levels and well-developed funds management practices. The institution has reliable access to sufficient sources of funds on favorable terms to meet present and anticipated liquidity needs.

2   A rating of 2 indicates satisfactory liquidity levels and funds management practices. The institution has access to sufficient sources of funds on acceptable terms to meet present and anticipated liquidity needs. Modest weaknesses may be evident in funds management practices.

3   A rating of 3 indicates liquidity levels or funds management practices in need of mprovement. Institutions rated 3 may lack ready access to funds on reasonable terms or may evidence significant weaknesses in funds management practices.

4   A rating of 4 indicates deficient liquidity levels or inadequate funds management practices. Institutions rated 4 may not have or be able to obtain a sufficient volume of funds on reasonable terms to meet liquidity needs.

5   A rating of 5 indicates liquidity levels or funds management practices so critically deficient that the continued viability of the institution is threatened. Institutions rated 5 require immediate external financial assistance to meet maturing obligations or other liquidity needs.

Sensitivity to Market Risk

The sensitivity to market risk component reflects the degree to which changes in interest rates, foreign exchange rates, commodity prices, or equity prices can adversely affect a financial institution's earnings or economic capital. When evaluating this component, consideration should be given to: management's ability to identify, measure, monitor, and control market risk; the institution's size; the nature and complexity of its activities; and the adequacy of its capital and earnings in relation to its level of market risk exposure.

For many institutions, the primary source of market risk arises from nontrading positions and their sensitivity to changes in interest rates. In some larger institutions, foreign operations can be a significant source of market risk. For some institutions, trading activities are a major source of market risk.

Market risk is rated based upon, but not limited to, an assessment of the following evaluation factors:

- The sensitivity of the financial institution's earnings or the economic value of its capital to adverse changes in interest rates, foreign exchanges rates, commodity prices, or equity prices.
- The ability of management to identify, measure, monitor, and control exposure to market risk given the institution's size, complexity, and risk profile.

- The nature and complexity of interest rate risk exposure arising from nontrading positions.
- If appropriate, the nature and complexity of market risk exposure arising from trading, asset management activities, and foreign operations.

Sensitivity to Market Risk Ratings

1 A rating of 1 indicates that market risk sensitivity is well controlled and that there is minimal potential that the earnings performance or capital position will be adversely affected. Risk management practices are strong for the size, sophistication, and market risk accepted by the institution. The level of earnings and capital provide substantial support for the amount of market risk taken by the institution.

2 A rating of 2 indicates that market risk sensitivity is adequately controlled and that there is only moderate potential that the earnings performance or capital position will be adversely affected. Risk management practices are satisfactory for the size, sophistication, and market risk accepted by the institution. The level of earnings and capital provide adequate support for the amount of market risk taken by the institution.

3 A rating of 3 indicates that control of market risk sensitivity needs improvement or that there is significant potential that the earnings performance or capital position will be adversely affected. Risk management practices need to be improved given the size, sophistication, and level of market risk accepted by the institution. The level of earnings and capital may not adequately support the amount of market risk taken by the institution.

4 A rating of 4 indicates that control of market risk sensitivity is unacceptable or that there is high potential that the earnings performance or capital position will be adversely affected. Risk management practices are deficient for the size, sophistication, and level of market risk accepted by the institution. The level of earnings and capital provide inadequate support for the amount of market risk taken by the institution.

5 A rating of 5 indicates that control of market risk sensitivity is unacceptable or that the level of market risk taken by the institution is an imminent threat to its viability. Risk management practices are wholly inadequate for the size, sophistication, and level of market risk accepted by the institution.

Appendix B: Information Technology Rating System

On January 13, 1999, the Federal Financial Institution Examination Council issued the Uniform Rating System for Information Technology (URSIT) to uniformly assess financial institution and service provider risks introduced by information technology.[46] URSIT replaced the prior rating system for information systems adopted in 1978.

Overview

The OCC implemented the URSIT rating system for all national banks and OCC-supervised service provider examinations that began after April 1, 1999. URSIT consists of a composite and four component ratings:

- Audit.
- Management.
- Development and acquisition.
- Support and delivery.

The OCC revised the application of URSIT for examinations that began after April 1, 2001. Examiners assign a composite-only rating to all national banks (including federal branches and agencies, national trust banks, credit card banks, and other special purpose banks) and their operating subsidiaries. Examiners continue to assign component ratings in the examination of technology service providers.[47] The change to a composite-only rating for national banks is consistent with the agency's move toward a more integrated, risk-based approach to IT examinations.

Under the integrated examination approach, examiners focus on the risk issues inherent in automated information systems, rather than the functional activities rated by the URSIT components. These risk issues, common to all automated systems, include:

- Management of technology resources, whether in-house or outsourced;

- Integrity of automated information (i.e., reliability of data and protection from unauthorized change);

- Availability of automated information (i.e., adequacy of business resumption and contingency planning); and

- Confidentiality of information (i.e., protection from accidental or inadvertent disclosure).

---

[46] Federal Register, Volume 64, No. 12, January 20, 1999, pages 3109-3116, Uniform Rating System for Information Technology.
[47] Refer to "Supervision of Technology Service Providers" booklet of the FFIEC IT Examination Handbook for guidance on examining and rating TSPs.

These common technology risk issues are used to assess the overall performance of IT within an organization. Examiners evaluate each issue to assess the institution's ability to identify, measure, monitor, and control IT risks. Each institution is then assigned an URSIT composite rating based on the overall results of the evaluation. The rating is based on a scale of "1" through "5" in ascending order of supervisory concern; "1" representing the best rating and least degree of concern, and "5" representing the worst rating and highest degree of concern.

Composite Ratings[48]

Composite 1

Financial institutions and service providers rated composite "1" exhibit strong performance in every respect. Weaknesses in IT are minor in nature and are easily corrected during the normal course of business. Risk management processes provide a comprehensive program to identify and monitor risk relative to the size, complexity and risk profile of the entity. Strategic plans are well defined and fully integrated throughout the organization. This allows management to quickly adapt to changing market, business and technology needs of the entity. Management identifies weaknesses promptly and takes appropriate corrective action to resolve audit and regulatory concerns. The financial condition of the service provider is strong and overall performance shows no cause for supervisory concern.

Composite 2

Financial institutions and service providers rated composite "2" exhibit safe and sound performance but may demonstrate modest weaknesses in operating performance, monitoring, management processes or system development. Generally, senior management corrects weaknesses in the normal course of business. Risk management processes adequately identify and monitor risk relative to the size, complexity and risk profile of the entity. Strategic plans are defined but may require clarification, better coordination or improved communication throughout the organization. As a result, management anticipates, but responds less quickly to changes in market, business, and technological needs of the entity. Management normally identifies weaknesses and takes appropriate corrective action. However, greater reliance is placed on audit and regulatory intervention to identify and resolve concerns. The financial condition of the service provider is acceptable and while internal control weaknesses may exist, there are no significant supervisory concerns. As a result, supervisory action is informal and limited.

Composite 3

Financial institutions and service providers rated composite "3" exhibit some degree of supervisory concern because of a combination of weaknesses that may range from moderate to severe. If weaknesses persist, further deterioration in the condition and performance of the institution or service provider is likely. Risk management processes may not effectively

---

[48] The descriptive examples in the numeric composite rating definitions are intended to provide guidance to examiners as they evaluate the overall condition of information technology. Examiners must use professional judgement when making this assessment and assigning the numeric rating.

identify risks and may not be appropriate for the size, complexity, or risk profile of the entity. Strategic plans are vaguely defined and may not provide adequate direction for IT initiatives. As a result, management often has difficulty responding to changes in business, market, and technological needs of the entity. Self-assessment practices are weak and are generally reactive to audit and regulatory exceptions. Repeat concerns may exist, indicating that management may lack the ability or willingness to resolve concerns. The financial condition of the service provider may be weak and/or negative trends may be evident. While financial or operational failure is unlikely, increased supervision is necessary. Formal or informal supervisory action may be necessary to secure corrective action.

Composite 4

Financial institutions and service providers rated composite "4" operate in an unsafe and unsound environment that may impair the future viability of the entity. Operating weaknesses are indicative of serious managerial deficiencies. Risk management processes inadequately identify and monitor risk, and practices are not appropriate given the size, complexity, and risk profile of the entity. Strategic plans are poorly defined and not coordinated or communicated throughout the organization. As a result, management and the board are not committed to meeting technological needs and may be incapable of meeting those needs. Management does not perform self-assessments and demonstrates an inability or unwillingness to correct audit and regulatory concerns. The financial condition of the service provider is severely impaired and/or deteriorating. Failure of the financial institution or service provider may be likely unless IT problems are remedied. Close supervisory attention is necessary and, in most cases, formal enforcement action is warranted.

Composite 5

Financial institutions and service providers rated composite "5" exhibit critically deficient operating performance and are in need of immediate remedial action. Operational problems and serious weaknesses may exist throughout the organization. Risk management processes are severely deficient and provide management little or no perception of risk relative to the size, complexity, and risk profile of the entity. Strategic plans do not exist or are ineffective, and management and the board provide little or no direction for IT initiatives. As a result, management is unaware of, or inattentive to technological needs of the entity. Management is unwilling to correct audit and regulatory concerns or is incapable of doing so. The financial condition of the service provider is poor and failure is highly probable because of poor operating performance or financial instability. Ongoing supervisory attention is necessary.

Appendix C: Trust Rating System

The Uniform Interagency Trust Rating System (UITRS) was adopted in 1978 and revised in 1998. The UITRS considers certain managerial, operational, financial, and compliance factors that are common to all institutions with fiduciary activities. Under this system, the supervisory agencies endeavor to ensure that all institutions with fiduciary activities are evaluated in a comprehensive and uniform manner, and that supervisory attention is appropriately focused on those institutions exhibiting weaknesses in their fiduciary operations.

Overview[49]

Under the UITRS, the fiduciary activities of financial institutions are assigned a composite rating based on an evaluation and rating of five essential components of an institution's fiduciary activities. These components are: the capability of management; the adequacy of operations, controls and audits; the quality and level of earnings; compliance with governing instruments, applicable law (including self-dealing and conflicts of interest laws and regulations), and sound fiduciary principles; and the management of fiduciary assets.

Composite and component ratings are assigned on a 1-to-5 numerical scale. A 1 is the highest rating and indicates the strongest performance and risk management practices and the least supervisory concern. A 5 is the lowest rating and indicates the weakest performance and risk management practices and, therefore, the greatest supervisory concern. Evaluation of the composite and components considers the size and sophistication, the nature and complexity, and the risk profile of the institution's fiduciary activities.

The composite rating generally bears a close relationship to the component ratings assigned. However, the composite rating is not derived by computing an arithmetic average of the component ratings. Each component rating is based on a qualitative analysis of the factors comprising that component and its interrelationship with the other components. When assigning a composite rating, some components may be given more weight than others depending on the situation at the institution. In general, assignment of a composite rating may incorporate any factor that bears significantly on the overall administration of the financial institution's fiduciary activities. Assigned composite and component ratings are disclosed to the institution's board of directors and senior management.

The ability of management to respond to changing circumstances and to address the risks that may arise from changing business conditions, or the initiation of new fiduciary activities or products, is an important factor in evaluating an institution's overall fiduciary risk profile and the level of supervisory attention warranted. For this reason, the management component is given special consideration when assigning a composite rating. The ability of management to identify, measure, monitor, and control the risks of its fiduciary operations is also taken into

---

[49] Excerpt taken from Federal Register, Volume 63, No. 197, October 13, 1998, pages 54704-54711, Uniform Interagency Trust Rating System.

account when assigning each component rating. It is recognized, however, that appropriate management practices may vary considerably among financial institutions, depending on the size, complexity and risk profiles of their fiduciary activities. For less complex institutions engaged solely in traditional fiduciary activities and whose directors and senior managers are actively involved in the oversight and management of day-to-day operations, relatively basic management systems and controls may be adequate. On the other hand, at more complex institutions, detailed and formal management systems and controls are needed to address a broader range of activities and to provide senior managers and directors with the information they need to supervise day-to-day activities.

All institutions are expected to properly manage their risks. For less complex institutions engaging in less risky activities, detailed or highly formalized management systems and controls are not required to receive strong or satisfactory component or composite ratings.

The following two sections contain the composite rating definitions, and the descriptions and definitions for the five component ratings.

Composite Ratings

Composite ratings are based on a careful evaluation of how an institution conducts its fiduciary activities. The review encompasses the capability of management, the soundness of policies and practices, the quality of service rendered to the public, and the effect of fiduciary activities upon the soundness of the institution. The five key components used to assess an institution's fiduciary activities are: the capability of management; the adequacy of operations, controls and audits; the quality and level of earnings; compliance with governing instruments, applicable law (including self-dealing and conflicts of interest laws and regulations), and sound fiduciary principles; and the management of fiduciary assets. The composite ratings are defined as follows:

Composite 1

Administration of fiduciary activities is sound in every respect. Generally all components are rated 1 or 2. Any weaknesses are minor and can be handled in a routine manner by management. The institution is in substantial compliance with fiduciary laws and regulations. Risk management practices are strong relative to the size, complexity, and risk profile of the institution's fiduciary activities. Fiduciary activities are conducted in accordance with sound fiduciary principles and give no cause for supervisory concern.

Composite 2

Administration of fiduciary activities is fundamentally sound. Generally no component rating should be more severe than 3. Only moderate weaknesses are present and are well within management's capabilities and willingness to correct. Fiduciary activities are conducted in substantial compliance with laws and regulations. Overall risk management practices are satisfactory relative to the institution's size, complexity, and risk profile. There are no material supervisory concerns and, as a result, the supervisory response is informal and limited.

Composite 3

Administration of fiduciary activities exhibits some degree of supervisory concern in one or more of the component areas. A combination of weaknesses exists that may range from moderate to severe; however, the magnitude of the deficiencies generally does not cause a component to be rated more severely than 4. Management may lack the ability or willingness to effectively address weaknesses within appropriate time frames. Additionally, fiduciary activities may reveal some significant noncompliance with laws and regulations. Risk management practices may be less than satisfactory relative to the institution's size, complexity, and risk profile. While problems of relative significance may exist, they are not of such importance as to pose a threat to the trust beneficiaries generally, or to the soundness of the institution. The institution's fiduciary activities require more than normal supervision and may include formal or informal enforcement actions.

Composite 4

Fiduciary activities generally exhibit unsafe and unsound practices or conditions, resulting in unsatisfactory performance. The problems range from severe to critically deficient and may be centered around inexperienced or inattentive management, weak or dangerous operating practices, or an accumulation of unsatisfactory features of lesser importance. The weaknesses and problems are not being satisfactorily addressed or resolved by the board of directors and management. There may be significant noncompliance with laws and regulations. Risk management practices are generally unacceptable relative to the size, complexity, and risk profile of fiduciary activities. These problems pose a threat to the account beneficiaries generally and, if left unchecked, could evolve into conditions that could cause significant losses to the institution and ultimately undermine the public confidence in the institution. Close supervisory attention is required, which means, in most cases, formal enforcement action is necessary to address the problems.

Composite 5

Fiduciary activities are conducted in an extremely unsafe and unsound manner. Administration of fiduciary activities is critically deficient in numerous major respects, with problems resulting from incompetent or neglectful administration, flagrant and/or repeated disregard for laws and regulations, or a willful departure from sound fiduciary principles and practices. The volume and severity of problems are beyond management's ability or willingness to control or correct. Such conditions evidence a flagrant disregard for the interests of the beneficiaries and may pose a serious threat to the soundness of the institution. Continuous close supervisory attention is warranted and may include termination of the institutions fiduciary activities.

Component Ratings

Each of the component rating descriptions is divided into three sections: a narrative description of the component; a list of the principal factors used to evaluate that component; and a description of each numerical rating for that component. Some of the evaluation factors are reiterated under one or more of the other components to reinforce the interrelationship among components. The listing of evaluation factors is in no particular order of importance.

Management

This rating reflects the capability of the board of directors and management, in their respective roles, to identify, measure, monitor and control the risks of an institution's fiduciary activities. It also reflects their ability to ensure that the institution's fiduciary activities are conducted in a safe and sound manner, and in compliance with applicable laws and regulations. Directors should provide clear guidance regarding acceptable risk exposure levels and ensure that appropriate policies, procedures and practices are established and followed. Senior fiduciary management is responsible for developing and implementing policies, procedures and practices that translate the board's objectives and risk limits into prudent operating standards.

Depending on the nature and scope of an institution's fiduciary activities, management practices may need to address some or all of the following risks: reputation, operating or transaction, strategic, compliance, legal, credit, market, liquidity and other risks. Sound management practices are demonstrated by: active oversight by the board of directors and management; competent personnel; adequate policies, processes, and controls that consider the size and complexity of the institution's fiduciary activities; and effective risk monitoring and management information systems. This rating should reflect the board's and management's ability as it applies to all aspects of fiduciary activities in which the institution is involved.

The management rating is based upon an assessment of the capability and performance of management and the board of directors, including, but not limited to, the following evaluation factors:

- The level and quality of oversight and support of fiduciary activities by the board of directors and management, including committee structure and adequate documentation of committee actions.

- The ability of the board of directors and management, in their respective roles, to plan for, and respond to, risks that may arise from changing business conditions or the introduction of new activities or products.

- The adequacy of, and conformance with, appropriate internal policies, practices and controls addressing the operations and risks of significant fiduciary activities.

- The accuracy, timeliness, and effectiveness of management information and risk monitoring systems appropriate for the institutions size, complexity, and fiduciary risk profile.

- The overall level of compliance with laws, regulations, and sound fiduciary principles.

- Responsiveness to recommendations from auditors and regulatory authorities.

- Strategic planning for fiduciary products and services.

- The level of experience and competence of fiduciary management and staff, including issues relating to turnover and succession planning.

- The adequacy of insurance coverage.

- The availability of competent legal counsel.

- The extent and nature of pending litigation associated with fiduciary activities, and its potential impact on earnings, capital, and the institution's reputation.

- The process for identifying and responding to fiduciary customer complaints.

Management Ratings

1 A rating of 1 indicates strong performance by management and the board of directors and strong risk management practices relative to the size, complexity and risk profile of the institution's fiduciary activities. All significant risks are consistently and effectively identified, measured, monitored, and controlled. Management and the board are proactive, and have demonstrated the ability to promptly and successfully address existing and potential problems and risks.

2 A rating of 2 indicates satisfactory management and board performance and risk management practices relative to the size, complexity and risk profile of the institution's fiduciary activities. Moderate weaknesses may exist, but are not material to the sound administration of fiduciary activities, and are being addressed. In general, significant risks and problems are effectively identified, measured, monitored, and controlled.

3 A rating of 3 indicates management and board performance that needs improvement or risk management practices that are less than satisfactory given the nature of the institution's fiduciary activities. The capabilities of management or the board of directors may be insufficient for the size, complexity, and risk profile of the institution's fiduciary activities. Problems and significant risks may be inadequately identified, measured, monitored, or controlled.

4 A rating of 4 indicates deficient management and board performance or risk management practices that are inadequate considering the size, complexity, and risk profile of the institution's fiduciary activities. The level of problems and risk exposure is excessive. Problems and significant risks are inadequately identified, measured, monitored, or controlled and require immediate action by the board and management to protect the assets of account beneficiaries and to prevent erosion of public confidence in the institution. Replacing or strengthening management or the board may be necessary.

5 A rating of 5 indicates critically deficient management and board performance or risk management practices. Management and the board of directors have not demonstrated the ability to correct problems and implement appropriate risk management practices. Problems and significant risks are inadequately identified, measured, monitored, or controlled and now threaten the continued viability of the institution or its administration of fiduciary activities, and pose a threat to the safety of the assets of account beneficiaries. Replacing or strengthening management or the board of directors is necessary.

Operations, Internal Controls & Auditing

This rating reflects the adequacy of the institution's fiduciary operating systems and internal controls in relation to the volume and character of business conducted. Audit coverage must assure the integrity of the financial records, the sufficiency of internal controls, and the adequacy of the compliance process.

The institution's fiduciary operating systems, internal controls, and audit function subject it primarily to transaction and compliance risk. Other risks including reputation, strategic, and financial risk may also be present. The ability of management to identify, measure, monitor and control these risks is reflected in this rating.

The operations, internal controls and auditing rating is based upon, but not limited to, an assessment of the following evaluation factors:

- *Operations and Internal Controls*, including the adequacy of
  - Staff, facilities and operating systems;
  - Records, accounting and data processing systems (including controls over systems access and such accounting procedures as aging, investigation and disposition of items in suspense accounts);
  - Trading functions and securities lending activities;
  - Vault controls and securities movement;
  - Segregation of duties;
  - Controls over disbursements (checks or electronic) and unissued securities;
  - Controls over income processing activities;
  - Reconciliation processes (depository, cash, vault, sub-custodians, suspense accounts, etc.);
  - Disaster and/or business recovery programs;

- Hold-mail procedures and controls over returned mail; and
- Investigation and proper escheatment of funds in dormant accounts.

- *Auditing*, including
  - The independence, frequency, quality and scope of the internal and external fiduciary audit function relative to the volume, character and risk profile of the institution's fiduciary activities;
  - The volume and/or severity of internal control and audit exceptions and the extent to which these issues are tracked and resolved; and
  - The experience and competence of the audit staff.

Operations, Internal Controls & Auditing Ratings

1   A rating of 1 indicates that operations, internal controls, and auditing are strong in relation to the volume and character of the institution's fiduciary activities. All significant risks are consistently and effectively identified, measured, monitored, and controlled.

2   A rating of 2 indicates that operations, internal controls and auditing are satisfactory in relation to the volume and character of the institution's fiduciary activities. Moderate weaknesses may exist, but are not material. Significant risks, in general, are effectively identified, measured, monitored, and controlled.

3   A rating of 3 indicates that operations, internal controls or auditing need improvement in relation to the volume and character of the institution fiduciary activities. One or more of these areas are less than satisfactory. Problems and significant risks may be inadequately identified, measured, monitored, or controlled.

4   A rating of 4 indicates deficient operations, internal controls or audits. One or more of these areas are inadequate or the level of problems and risk exposure is excessive in relation to the volume and character of the institution's fiduciary activities. Problems and significant risks are inadequately identified, measured, monitored, or controlled and require immediate action. Institutions with this level of deficiencies may make little provision for audits, or may evidence weak or potentially dangerous operating practices in combination with infrequent or inadequate audits.

5   A rating of 5 indicates critically deficient operations, internal controls or audits. Operating practices, with or without audits, pose a serious threat to the safety of assets of fiduciary accounts. Problems and significant risks are inadequately identified, measured, monitored, or controlled and now threaten the ability of the institution to continue engaging in fiduciary activities.

Earnings[50]

This rating reflects the profitability of an institution's fiduciary activities and its effect on the financial condition of the institution. The use and adequacy of budgets and earnings projections by functions, product lines, and clients are reviewed and evaluated. Risk exposure that may lead to negative earnings is also evaluated.

An evaluation of earnings is required for all institutions with fiduciary activities. An assignment of an earnings rating, however, is required only for institutions that, at the time of the examination, have total trust assets of more than $100 million, or are non-deposit trust companies (those institutions that would be required to file Schedule E of FFIEC 001).

If the UITRS does not require that a particular institution receive an earnings rating, the federal supervisory agency has the option to assign an earnings rating using an alternate set of ratings. A rating will be assigned in accordance with implementing guidelines adopted by the supervisory agency. The definitions for the alternate ratings are included in the revised UITRS and may be found in the section immediately following the definitions for the required ratings.

The evaluation of earnings is based upon, but not limited to, an assessment of the following factors:

- The profitability of fiduciary activities in relation to the size and scope of those activities and to the overall business of the institution.
- The overall importance to the institution of offering fiduciary services to its customers and local community.
- The effectiveness of the institution's procedures for monitoring fiduciary activity income and expense relative to the size and scope of these activities and their relative importance to the institution, including the frequency and scope of profitability reviews and planning by the institution's board of directors or a committee thereof.

For those institutions that must receive an earnings rating, additional factors should include

- The level and consistency of profitability, or the lack thereof, generated by the institution's fiduciary activities in relation to the volume and character of the institution's business.
- Dependence upon non-recurring fees and commissions, such as fees for court accounts.
- The effect of charge-offs or compromise actions.
- Unusual features regarding the composition of business and fee schedules.

---

[50] The OCC will not require an earnings rating to be assigned at institutions when an earnings component rating is not required under the UITRS. For these institutions, an evaluation of fiduciary earnings should be forwarded to the bank EIC for consideration in assigning the UFIRS earnings component rating.

- Accounting practices that contain practices such as (1) unusual methods of allocating direct and indirect expenses and overhead, or (2) unusual methods of allocating fiduciary income and expense where two or more fiduciary institutions within the same holding company family share fiduciary services and/or processing functions.
- The extent of management's use of budgets, projections and other cost analysis procedures.
- Methods used for directors' approval of financial budgets and/or projections.
- Management's attitude toward growth and new business development.
- New business development efforts, including types of business solicited, market potential, advertising, competition, relationships with local organizations, and an evaluation by management of risk potential inherent in new business areas.

Earnings Ratings

1   A rating of 1 indicates strong earnings. The institution consistently earns a rate of return on its fiduciary activities that is commensurate with the risk of those activities. This rating would normally be supported by a history of consistent profitability over time and a judgment that future earnings prospects are favorable. In addition, management techniques for evaluating and monitoring earnings performance are fully adequate and there is appropriate oversight by the institution's board of directors or a committee thereof. Management makes effective use of budgets and cost analysis procedures. Methods used for reporting earnings information to the board of directors, or a committee thereof, are comprehensive.

2   A rating of 2 indicates satisfactory earnings. Although the earnings record may exhibit some weaknesses, earnings performance does not pose a risk to the overall institution nor to its ability to meet its fiduciary obligations. Generally, fiduciary earnings meet management targets and appear to be at least sustainable. Management processes for evaluating and monitoring earnings are generally sufficient in relationship to the size and risk of fiduciary activities that exist, and any deficiencies can be addressed in the normal course of business. A rating of 2 may also be assigned to institutions with a history of profitable operations if there are indications that management is engaging in activities with which it is not familiar, or where there may be inordinately high levels of risk present that have not been adequately evaluated. Alternatively, an institution with otherwise strong earnings performance may also be assigned a 2 rating if there are significant deficiencies in its methods used to monitor and evaluate earnings.

3   A rating of 3 indicates less than satisfactory earnings. Earnings are not commensurate with the risk associated with the fiduciary activities undertaken. Earnings may be erratic or exhibit downward trends and future prospects are unfavorable. This rating may also be assigned if management processes for evaluating and monitoring earnings exhibit serious deficiencies, provided the deficiencies identified do not pose an immediate danger to either the overall financial condition of the institution or its ability to meet its fiduciary obligations.

4   A rating of 4 indicates earnings that are seriously deficient. Fiduciary activities have a significant adverse effect on the overall income of the institution and its ability to

generate adequate capital to support the continued operation of its fiduciary activities. The institution is characterized by fiduciary earnings performance that is poor historically, or faces the prospect of significant losses in the future. Management processes for monitoring and evaluating earnings may be poor. The board of directors has not adopted appropriate measures to address significant deficiencies.

5   A rating of 5 indicates critically deficient earnings. In general, an institution with this rating is experiencing losses from fiduciary activities that have a significant negative impact on the overall institution, representing a distinct threat to its viability through the erosion of its capital. The board of directors has not implemented effective actions to address the situation.

Alternate Rating of Earnings

Alternate ratings are assigned based on the level of implementation of four minimum standards by the board of directors and management. These standards are

- Standard No. 1—The institution has reasonable methods for measuring income and expense commensurate with the volume and nature of the fiduciary services offered.
- Standard No. 2—The level of profitability is reported to the board of directors, or a committee thereof, at least annually.
- Standard No. 3—The board of directors periodically determines that the continued offering of fiduciary services provides an essential service to the institution's customers or to the local community.
- Standard No. 4—The board of directors, or a committee thereof, reviews the justification for the institution to continue to offer fiduciary services even if the institution does not earn sufficient income to cover the expenses of providing those services.

Alternative Earnings Ratings

1   A rating of 1 may be assigned where an institution has implemented all four minimum standards. If fiduciary earnings are lacking, management views this as a cost of doing business as a full service institution and believes that the negative effects of not offering fiduciary services are more significant than the expense of administrating those services.

2   A rating of 2 may be assigned to an institution that has implemented, at least three of the four standards. This rating may be assigned if the institution is not generating positive earnings or where formal earnings information may not be available.

3   A rating of 3 may be assigned to the institution that has implemented at least two of the four standards. While management may have attempted to identify and quantify other revenue to be earned by offering fiduciary services, it has decided that these services should be offered as a service to customers, even if they cannot be operated profitably.

4   A rating of 4 may be assigned to an institution that has implemented only one of the four standards. Management has undertaken little or no effort to identify or quantify the collateral advantages, if any, to the institution from offering fiduciary services.

5   A rating of 5 may be assigned if the institution has implemented none of the standards.

Compliance

This rating reflects an institution's overall compliance with applicable laws, regulations, accepted standards of fiduciary conduct, governing account instruments, duties associated with account administration, and internally established policies and procedures. This component specifically incorporates an assessment of a fiduciary's duty of undivided loyalty and compliance with applicable laws, regulations, and accepted standards of fiduciary conduct related to self-dealing and other conflicts of interest.

The compliance component includes reviewing and evaluating the adequacy and soundness of adopted policies, procedures, and practices generally, and as they relate to specific transactions and accounts. It also includes reviewing policies, procedures, and practices to evaluate how committed management and the board of directors are to refraining from self-dealing, minimizing potential conflicts of interest, and resolving actual conflict situations in favor of the fiduciary account beneficiaries.

Risks associated with account administration are potentially unlimited because each account is a separate contractual relationship that contains specific obligations. Risks associated with account administration include: failure to comply with applicable laws, regulations or terms of the governing instrument; inadequate account administration practices; and inexperienced management or inadequately trained staff. Risks associated with a fiduciary's duty of undivided loyalty generally stem from engaging in self-dealing or other conflict of interest transactions. An institution may be exposed to compliance, strategic, financial and reputation risk related to account administration and conflicts of interest activities. The ability of management to identify, measure, monitor and control these risks is reflected in this rating. Policies, procedures and practices pertaining to account administration and conflicts of interest are evaluated in light of the size and character of an institution's fiduciary business.

The compliance rating is based upon, but not limited to, an assessment of the following evaluation factors:

- Compliance with applicable federal and state statutes and regulations, including, but not limited to, federal and state fiduciary laws, the Employee Retirement Income Security Act of 1974, federal and state securities laws, state investment standards, state principal and income acts, and state probate codes;
- Compliance with the terms of governing instruments;
- The adequacy of overall policies, practices, and procedures governing compliance, considering the size, complexity, and risk profile of the institutions fiduciary activities;
- The adequacy of policies and procedures addressing account administration;
- The adequacy of policies and procedures addressing conflicts of interest, including those designed to prevent the improper use of "material inside information";
- The effectiveness of systems and controls in place to identify actual and potential conflicts of interest;

- The adequacy of securities trading policies and practices relating to the allocation of brokerage business, the payment of services with "soft dollars" and the combining, crossing, and timing of trades;
- The extent and permissibility of transactions with related parties, including, but not limited to, the volume of related commercial and fiduciary relationships and holdings of corporations in which directors, officers, or employees of the institution may be interested;
- The decision-making process used to accept, review, and terminate accounts; and
- The decision-making process related to account administration duties, including cash balances, overdrafts, and discretionary distributions.

Compliance Ratings

1   A rating of 1 indicates strong compliance policies, procedures and practices. Policies and procedures covering conflicts of interest and account administration are appropriate in relation to the size and complexity of the institution's fiduciary activities. Accounts are administered in accordance with governing instruments, applicable laws and regulations, sound fiduciary principles, and internal policies and procedures. Any violations are isolated, technical in nature and easily correctable. All significant risks are consistently and effectively identified, measured, monitored and controlled.

2   A rating of 2 indicates fundamentally sound compliance policies, procedures and practices in relation to the size and complexity of the institution's fiduciary activities. Account administration may be flawed by moderate weaknesses in policies, procedures or practices. Management's practices indicate a determination to minimize the instances of conflicts of interest. Fiduciary activities are conducted in substantial compliance with laws and regulations, and any violations are generally technical in nature. Management corrects violations in a timely manner and without loss to fiduciary accounts. Significant risks are effectively identified, measured, monitored, and controlled.

3   A rating of 3 indicates compliance practices that are less than satisfactory in relation to the size and complexity of the institution's fiduciary activities. Policies, procedures and controls have not proven effective and require strengthening. Fiduciary activities may be in substantial noncompliance with laws, regulations, or governing instruments, but losses are no worse than minimal. While management may have the ability to achieve compliance, the number of violations that exist, or the failure to correct prior violations, are indications that management has not devoted sufficient time and attention to its compliance responsibilities. Risk management practices generally need improvement.

4   A rating of 4 indicates an institution with deficient compliance practices in relation to the size and complexity of its fiduciary activities. Account administration is notably deficient. The institution makes little or no effort to minimize potential conflicts or refrain from self-dealing, and is confronted with a considerable number of potential or actual conflicts. Numerous substantive and technical violations of laws and regulations exist and many may remain uncorrected from previous examinations. Management has not exerted sufficient effort to effect compliance and may lack the ability to effectively

administer fiduciary activities. The level of compliance problems is significant and, if left unchecked, may subject the institution to monetary losses or reputation risk. Risks are inadequately identified, measured, monitored and controlled.

5   A rating of 5 indicates critically deficient compliance practices. Account administration is critically deficient or incompetent and there is a flagrant disregard for the terms of the governing instruments and interests of account beneficiaries. The institution frequently engages in transactions that compromise its fundamental duty of undivided loyalty to account beneficiaries. There are flagrant or repeated violations of laws and regulations and significant departures from sound fiduciary principles. Management is unwilling or unable to operate within the scope of laws and regulations or within the terms of governing instruments and efforts to obtain voluntary compliance have been unsuccessful. The severity of noncompliance presents an imminent monetary threat to account beneficiaries and creates significant legal and financial exposure to the institution. Problems and significant risks are inadequately identified, measured, monitored, or controlled and now threaten the ability of management to continue engaging in fiduciary activities.

Asset Management[51]

This rating reflects the risks associated with managing the assets (including cash) of others. Prudent portfolio management is based on an assessment of the needs and objectives of each account or portfolio. An evaluation of asset management should consider the adequacy of processes related to the investment of all discretionary accounts and portfolios, including collective investment funds, proprietary mutual funds, and investment advisory arrangements.

The institution's asset management activities subject it to reputation, compliance and strategic risks. In addition, each individual account or portfolio managed by the institution is subject to financial risks such as market, credit, liquidity, and interest rate risk, as well as transaction and compliance risk. The ability of management to identify, measure, monitor and control these risks is reflected in this rating.

The asset management rating is based upon, but not limited to, an assessment of the following evaluation factors:

- The adequacy of overall policies, practices and procedures governing asset management, considering the size, complexity and risk profile of the institution's fiduciary activities.
- The decision-making processes used for selection, retention and preservation of discretionary assets including adequacy of documentation, committee review and approval, and a system to review and approve exceptions.
- The use of quantitative tools to measure the various financial risks in investment accounts and portfolios.

---

[51] The OCC will waive the asset management component rating only if the institution's fiduciary activities do not include managing or advising fiduciary account assets.

- The existence of policies and procedures addressing the use of derivatives or other complex investment products.
- The adequacy of procedures related to the purchase or retention of miscellaneous assets including real estate, notes, closely held companies, limited partnerships, mineral interests, insurance and other unique assets.
- The extent and adequacy of periodic reviews of investment performance, taking into consideration the needs and objectives of each account or portfolio.
- The monitoring of changes in the composition of fiduciary assets for trends and related risk exposure.
- The quality of investment research used in the decision-making process and documentation of the research.
- The due diligence process for evaluating investment advice received from vendors and/or brokers (including approved or focus lists of securities).
- The due diligence process for reviewing and approving brokers and/or counterparties used by the institution.

This rating may not be applicable for some institutions because their operations do not include activities involving the management of any discretionary assets. Functions of this type would include, but not necessarily be limited to, directed agency relationships, securities clearing, non-fiduciary custody relationships, transfer agent and registrar activities. In institutions of this type, the examiner may omit the rating for asset management in accordance with the examining agency's implementing guidelines. However, this component should be assigned when the institution provides investment advice, even though it does not have discretion over the account assets. An example of this type of activity would be where the institution selects or recommends the menu of mutual funds offered to participant directed 401(k) plans.

Asset Management Ratings

1   A rating of 1 indicates strong asset management practices. Identified weaknesses are minor in nature. Risk exposure is modest in relation to management's abilities and the size and complexity of the assets managed.

2   A rating of 2 indicates satisfactory asset management practices. Moderate weaknesses are present and are well within management's ability and willingness to correct. Risk exposure is commensurate with management's abilities and the size and complexity of the assets managed. Supervisory response is limited.

3   A rating of 3 indicates that asset management practices are less than satisfactory in relation to the size and complexity of the assets managed. Weaknesses may range from moderate to severe; however, they are not of such significance as to generally pose a threat to the interests of account beneficiaries. Asset management and risk management practices generally need to be improved. An elevated level of supervision is normally required.

4 A rating of 4 indicates deficient asset management practices in relation to the size and complexity of the assets managed. The levels of risk are significant and inadequately controlled. The problems pose a threat to account beneficiaries generally, and if left unchecked, may subject the institution to losses and could undermine the reputation of the institution.

5 A rating of 5 represents critically deficient asset management practices and a flagrant disregard of fiduciary duties. These practices jeopardize the interests of account beneficiaries, subject the institution to losses, and may pose a threat to the soundness of the institution.

Appendix D: Consumer Compliance Rating System

At the recommendation of the Federal Financial Institutions Examination Council, the federal banking regulatory agencies adopted the Uniform Interagency Consumer Compliance Rating System. The rating system is meant to reflect, in a comprehensive and uniform fashion, the nature and extent of an institution's compliance with consumer protection and civil rights statutes and regulations. The system helps identify institutions displaying compliance weaknesses requiring special supervisory attention.

The rating system provides a general framework for evaluating and integrating significant compliance factors to assign a consumer compliance rating to each institution. The rating system does not consider an institution's record of lending performance under the Community Reinvestment Act (CRA) or its compliance with the applicable provisions of the implementing regulations. Compliance with the CRA is rated separately.

Overview[52]

Under the uniform rating system, each financial institution is assigned a consumer compliance rating based on an evaluation of its present compliance with consumer protection and civil rights statutes and regulations and the adequacy of its operating systems designed to ensure continuing compliance. Ratings are given on a scale of 1 through 5 in increasing order of supervisory concern. Thus, 1 represents the highest rating and consequently the lowest level of supervisory concern; while 5 represents the lowest, most critically deficient level of performance and, therefore, the highest degree of supervisory concern.

In assigning a consumer compliance rating, all relevant factors must be evaluated. In general, those factors include

- The nature and extent of present compliance with consumer protection and civil rights statutes and regulations;
- The commitment of management to compliance and their ability and willingness to assure continuing compliance; and
- The adequacy of operating systems, including internal procedures, controls, and audit activities, designed to ensure compliance on a routine and consistent basis.

The assignment of a compliance rating may incorporate other factors that significantly affect the overall effectiveness of an institution's compliance efforts.

Although each financial institution differs in its general business powers and constraints, all are subject to the same consumer protection and civil rights laws and regulations covered by the rating system. Thus, there is no need to evaluate differing types of financial institutions on criteria relating to their particular industry. As a result, the assignment of a uniform

---

[52] Excerpt from the Uniform Interagency Consumer Compliance Rating System and the accompanying FFIEC Press Release dated November 18, 1980.

consumer compliance rating will help direct consistent supervisory attention that does not depend solely upon the nature of the institution's charter or business or the identity of its primary federal regulator. In this manner, overall uniformity and consistency of supervision will be strengthened by the existence of common consumer compliance ratings.

The uniform rating system is intended to help identify those institutions whose compliance with consumer protection and civil rights laws and regulations show weaknesses requiring special supervisory attention and which are cause for more than a normal degree of supervisory concern. To accomplish that objective, the rating system identifies an initial category of institutions that have compliance deficiencies that warrant more than normal supervisory concern. Those institutions are not deemed to present a significant risk of financial or other harm to consumers, but do require a higher than normal level of supervisory attention. Institutions in this category are generally rated 3. The rating system also identifies certain institutions whose weaknesses are so severe as to represent, in essence, a substantial or general disregard for the law. Those institutions, depending upon the nature and degree of their weaknesses, are rated 4 or 5.

Uniformly identifying institutions that give cause for more than a normal degree of supervisory concern will help ensure

- That the degree of supervisory attention and the type of supervisory response are based upon the severity and nature of the institution's problems;

- That supervisory attention and action are, to the extent possible, administered uniformly and consistently, regardless of the type of institution or the identity of the regulatory agency; and

- That appropriate supervisory action is taken for those institutions whose compliance problems entail the greatest potential for financial or other harm to consumers.

Consumer Compliance Ratings

Consumer compliance ratings are defined as follows:

1 An institution rated 1 is in a strong compliance position. Management is capable of and staff is sufficient for effectuating compliance. An effective compliance program, including an efficient system of internal procedures and controls, has been established. Changes in consumer statutes and regulations are promptly reflected in the institution's policies, procedures, and compliance training. The institution provides adequate training for its employees. If any violations are noted, they are relatively minor deficiencies in forms or practices and are easily corrected. There is no evidence of discriminatory acts or practices, reimbursable violations, or practices resulting in repeat violations. Violations and deficiencies are promptly corrected by management. As a result, the institution gives no cause for supervisory concern.

2   An institution rated 2 is in a generally strong compliance position. Management is capable of administering an effective compliance program. Although a system of internal operating procedures and controls has been established to ensure compliance, violations have nonetheless occurred. Those violations, however, involve technical aspects of the law or result from oversight on the part of operating personnel. Modifying the institution's compliance program or establishing additional review/audit procedures may eliminate many of the violations. Compliance training is satisfactory. There is no evidence of discriminatory acts or practices, reimbursable violations, or practices resulting in repeat violations.

3   Generally, an institution rated 3 is in a less-than-satisfactory compliance position. It is cause for supervisory concern and requires more than normal supervision to remedy deficiencies. Violations may be numerous. In addition, previously identified practices resulting in violations may remain uncorrected. Overcharges, if present, involve a few consumers and are minimal in amount. There is no evidence of discriminatory acts or practices. Although management may have the ability to effectuate compliance, increased efforts are necessary. The numerous violations discovered indicate that management has not devoted sufficient time and attention to consumer compliance. Operating procedures and controls have not proven effective and require strengthening by, among other things, designating a compliance officer and developing and implementing a comprehensive and effective compliance program. By identifying such an institution early, additional supervisory measures may be employed to eliminate violations and prevent further deterioration in the institution's less-than-satisfactory compliance position.

4   An institution rated 4 requires close supervisory attention and monitoring to promptly correct the serious compliance problems disclosed. Numerous violations are present. Overcharges, if any, affect a significant number of consumers and involve a substantial amount of money. Often practices resulting in violations and cited at previous examinations remain uncorrected. Discriminatory acts or practices may be in evidence. Clearly, management has not exerted sufficient effort to ensure compliance. Their attitude may indicate a lack of interest in administering an effective compliance program that may have contributed to the seriousness of the institution's compliance problems. Internal procedures and controls have not proven effective and are seriously deficient. Prompt action on the part of the supervisory agency may enable the institution to correct its deficiencies and improve its compliance position.

5   An institution rated 5 needs the strongest supervisory attention and monitoring. It is substantially in noncompliance with consumer laws and regulations. Management has demonstrated their unwillingness or inability to operate within the scope of consumer laws and regulations. Previous efforts on the part of the regulatory authority to obtain voluntary compliance have been unproductive. Discrimination, substantial overcharges, or practices resulting in serious repeat violations are present.

Appendix E: Community Reinvestment Act Rating System

The Community Reinvestment Act requires each appropriate federal financial supervisory agency to assess an institution's record of helping meet the credit needs of its entire community, including low- and moderate-income neighborhoods, consistent with the safe and sound operation of the institution.

In assigning a rating under the Community Reinvestment Act Rating System, the OCC evaluates a bank's performance under the applicable performance criteria outlined in 12 CFR 25, which provides for adjustments on the basis of evidence of discriminatory or other illegal credit practices. A bank's performance need not fit each aspect of a particular rating profile in order to receive that rating, and exceptionally strong performance with respect to some aspects may compensate for weak performance in others. The bank's overall performance, however, must be consistent with safe and sound banking practices and generally with the appropriate rating profile.

The OCC assigns to a bank a rating of "outstanding," "satisfactory," "needs to improve," or "substantial noncompliance" based on the bank's performance under the lending, investment and services tests, the community development test (for wholesale or limited purpose banks), the small and intermediate small bank performance standards, or an approved strategic plan, as applicable.

Lending, Investment, and Services Tests[53]

The OCC assigns a rating for a bank assessed under the lending, investment, and service tests in accordance with the following principles:

- A bank that receives an "outstanding" rating on the lending test receives an assigned rating of at least "satisfactory."
- A bank that receives an "outstanding" rating on both the service test and the investment test and a rating of at least "high satisfactory" on the lending test receives an assigned rating of "outstanding;" and
- No bank may receive an assigned rating of "satisfactory" or higher unless it receives a rating of at least "low satisfactory" on the lending test.

Lending Performance

The OCC assigns each bank's lending performance one of the five following ratings:

---

[53] Also known as the large bank performance criteria, the OCC applies these tests in evaluating the performance of a bank, unless the bank: is a wholesale or limited purpose bank; is a small bank, unless it elects to be evaluated under one of the other performance tests and standards; or submits, and the OCC approves, a strategic plan.

Outstanding

- Excellent responsiveness to credit needs in its assessment area(s), taking into account the number and amount of home mortgage, small business, small farm, and consumer loans, if applicable, in its assessment area(s);
- A substantial majority of its loans are made in its assessment area(s);
- An excellent geographic distribution of loans in its assessment area(s);
- An excellent distribution, particularly in its assessment area(s), of loans among individuals of different income levels and businesses (including farms) of different sizes, given the product lines offered by the bank;
- An excellent record of serving the credit needs of highly economically disadvantaged areas in its assessment area(s), low-income individuals, or businesses (including farms) with gross annual revenues of $1 million or less, consistent with safe and sound operations;
- Extensive use of innovative or flexible lending practices in a safe and sound manner to address the credit needs of low- or moderate-income individuals or geographies; and
- It is a leader in making community development loans.

High Satisfactory

- Good responsiveness to credit needs in its assessment area(s), taking into account the number and amount of home mortgage, small business, small farm, and consumer loans, if applicable, in its assessment area(s);
- A high percentage of its loans are made in its assessment area(s);
- A good geographic distribution of loans in its assessment area(s);
- A good distribution, particularly in its assessment area(s), of loans among individuals of different income levels and businesses (including farms) of different sizes, given the product lines offered by the bank;
- A good record of serving the credit needs of highly economically disadvantaged areas in its assessment area(s), low-income individuals, or businesses (including farms) with gross annual revenues of $1 million or less, consistent with safe and sound operations;
- Use of innovative or flexible lending practices in a safe and sound manner to address the credit needs of low- or moderate-income individuals or geographies; and
- It has made a relatively high level of community development loans.

Low Satisfactory

- Adequate responsiveness to credit needs in its assessment area(s), taking into account the number and amount of home mortgage, small business, small farm, and consumer loans, if applicable, in its assessment area(s);
- An adequate percentage of its loans are made in its assessment area(s);
- An adequate geographic distribution of loans in its assessment area(s);
- An adequate distribution, particularly in its assessment area(s), of loans among individuals of different income levels and businesses (including farms) of different sizes, given the product lines offered by the bank;

- An adequate record of serving the credit needs of highly economically disadvantaged areas in its assessment area(s), low-income individuals, or businesses (including farms) with gross annual revenues of $1 million or less, consistent with safe and sound operations;
- Limited use of innovative or flexible lending practices in a safe and sound manner to address the credit needs of low- or moderate-income individuals or geographies; and
- It has made an adequate level of community development loans.

Needs to Improve

- Poor responsiveness to credit needs in its assessment area(s), taking into account the number and amount of home mortgage, small business, small farm, and consumer loans, if applicable, in its assessment area(s);
- A small percentage of its loans are made in its assessment area(s);
- A poor geographic distribution of loans, particularly to low- or moderate-income geographies, in its assessment area(s);
- A poor distribution, particularly in its assessment area(s), of loans among individuals of different income levels and businesses (including farms) of different sizes, given the product lines offered by the bank;
- A poor record of serving the credit needs of highly economically disadvantaged areas in its assessment area(s), low-income individuals, or businesses (including farms) with gross annual revenues of $1 million or less, consistent with safe and sound operations;
- Little use of innovative or flexible lending practices in a safe and sound manner to address the credit needs of low- or moderate-income individuals or geographies; and
- It has made a low level of community development loans.

Substantial Noncompliance

- A very poor responsiveness to credit needs in its assessment area(s), taking into account the number and amount of home mortgage, small business, small farm, and consumer loans, if applicable, in its assessment area(s);
- A very small percentage of its loans are made in its assessment area(s);
- A very poor geographic distribution of loans, particularly to low- or moderate-income geographies, in its assessment area(s);
- A very poor distribution, particularly in its assessment area(s), of loans among individuals of different income levels and businesses (including farms) of different sizes, given the product lines offered by the bank;
- A very poor record of serving the credit needs of highly economically disadvantaged areas in its assessment area(s), low-income individuals, or businesses (including farms) with gross annual revenues of $1 million or less, consistent with safe and sound operations;
- No use of innovative or flexible lending practices in a safe and sound manner to address the credit needs of low- or moderate-income individuals or geographies; and
- It has made few, if any, community development loans.

Investment Performance

The OCC assigns each bank's investment performance one of the five following ratings:

Outstanding

An excellent level of qualified investments, particularly those that are not routinely provided by private investors, often in a leadership position;
Extensive use of innovative or complex qualified investments; and
Excellent responsiveness to credit and community development needs.

- A significant level of qualified investments, particularly those that are not routinely provided by private investors, occasionally in a leadership position;
- Significant use of innovative or complex qualified investments; and
- Good responsiveness to credit and community development needs.

Low Satisfactory

- An adequate level of qualified investments, particularly those that are not routinely provided by private investors, although rarely in a leadership position;
- Occasional use of innovative or complex qualified investments; and
- Adequate responsiveness to credit and community development needs.

Needs to Improve

- A poor level of qualified investments, particularly those that are not routinely provided by private investors;
- Rare use of innovative or complex qualified investments; and
- Poor responsiveness to credit and community development needs.

Substantial Noncompliance

- Few, if any, qualified investments, particularly those that are not routinely provided by private investors;
- No use of innovative or complex qualified investments; and
- Very poor responsiveness to credit and community development needs.

Service Performance

The OCC assigns each bank's service performance one of the five following ratings:

Outstanding

- Its service delivery systems are readily accessible to geographies and individuals of different income levels in its assessment area(s);

- To the extent changes have been made, its record of opening and closing branches has improved the accessibility of its delivery systems, particularly in low- or moderate-income geographies or to low- or moderate-income individuals;
- Its services (including, when appropriate, business hours) are tailored to the convenience and needs of its assessment area(s), particularly low- or moderate-income geographies or low- or moderate-income individuals; and
- It is a leader in providing community development services.

High Satisfactory

- Its service delivery systems are accessible to geographies and individuals of different income levels in its assessment area(s);
- To the extent changes have been made, its record of opening and closing branches has not adversely affected the accessibility of its delivery systems, particularly in low- and moderate-income geographies and to low- and moderate-income individuals;
- Its services (including, when appropriate, business hours) do not vary in a way that inconveniences its assessment area(s), particularly low- and moderate-income geographies and low- and moderate-income individuals; and
- It provides a relatively high level of community development services.

Low Satisfactory

- Its service delivery systems are reasonably accessible to geographies and individuals of different income levels in its assessment area(s);
- To the extent changes have been made, its record of opening and closing branches has generally not adversely affected the accessibility of its delivery systems, particularly in low- and moderate-income geographies and to low- and moderate-income individuals;
- Its services (including, when appropriate, business hours) do not vary in a way that inconveniences its assessment area(s), particularly low- and moderate-income geographies and low- and moderate-income individuals; and
- It provides an adequate level of community development services.

Needs to Improve

- Its service delivery systems are unreasonably inaccessible to portions of its assessment area(s), particularly to low- or moderate-income geographies or to low- or moderate-income individuals;
- To the extent changes have been made, its record of opening and closing branches has adversely affected the accessibility of its delivery systems, particularly in low- or moderate-income geographies or to low- or moderate-income individuals;
- Its services (including, when appropriate, business hours) vary in a way that inconveniences its assessment area(s), particularly low- or moderate-income geographies or low- or moderate-income individuals; and
- It provides a limited level of community development services.

Substantial Noncompliance

- Its service delivery systems are unreasonably inaccessible to significant portions of its assessment area(s), particularly to low- or moderate-income geographies or to low- or moderate-income individuals;
- To the extent changes have been made, its record of opening and closing branches has significantly adversely affected the accessibility of its delivery systems, particularly in low- or moderate-income geographies or to low- or moderate-income individuals;
- Its services (including, when appropriate, business hours) vary in a way that significantly inconveniences its assessment area(s), particularly low- or moderate-income geographies or low- or moderate-income individuals; and
- It provides few, if any, community development services.

Wholesale or Limited Purpose Banks

The OCC assigns each wholesale or limited purpose bank's community development performance one of the four following ratings:

Outstanding

- A high level of community development loans, community development services, or qualified investments, particularly investments that are not routinely provided by private investors;
- Extensive use of innovative or complex qualified investments, community development loans, or community development services; and
- Excellent responsiveness to credit and community development needs in its assessment area(s).

Satisfactory

- An adequate level of community development loans, community development services, or qualified investments, particularly investments that are not routinely provided by private investors;
- Occasional use of innovative or complex qualified investments, community development loans, or community development services; and
- Adequate responsiveness to credit and community development needs in its assessment area(s).

Needs to Improve

- A poor level of community development loans, community development services, or qualified investments, particularly investments that are not routinely provided by private investors;
- Rare use of innovative or complex qualified investments, community development loans, or community development services; and

- Poor responsiveness to credit and community development needs in its assessment area(s).

Substantial Noncompliance

- Few, if any, community development loans, community development services, or qualified investments, particularly investments that are not routinely provided by private investors;
- No use of innovative or complex qualified investments, community development loans, or community development services; and
- Very poor responsiveness to credit and community development needs in its assessment area(s).

Small and Intermediate Small Bank Performance Standards

Overall Rating for Small Banks

The OCC assigns an overall CRA rating for a bank assessed under the small bank performance standards based on the lending test.

Outstanding

A small bank that is not an intermediate small bank that meets each of the standards for a Satisfactory rating under the lending test and exceeds some or all of those standards may warrant consideration for an overall rating of Outstanding. In assessing whether a bank's performance is Outstanding, the OCC considers the extent to which the bank exceeds each of the performance standards for a Satisfactory rating and its performance in making qualified investments and its performance in providing branches and other services and delivery systems that enhance credit availability in its assessment area(s). These additional factors may increase a small bank's overall rating from Satisfactory to Outstanding, but could not compensate for a Needs to Improve lending test rating.

Needs to Improve or Substantial Noncompliance

A small bank may also receive a rating of Needs to Improve or Substantial Noncompliance depending on the degree to which its performance has failed to meet the standards for a Satisfactory rating.

Overall Rating for Intermediate Small Banks

The OCC assigns an overall CRA rating for a bank assessed under the intermediate small bank performance standards based on the lending test and the community development test.

Outstanding

An intermediate small bank that receives an Outstanding rating on one test and at least Satisfactory on the other test may receive an assigned overall rating of Outstanding.

Satisfactory

No intermediate small bank may receive an assigned overall rating of Satisfactory unless it receives a rating of at least Satisfactory on both the lending test and the community development test.

Needs to Improve or Substantial Noncompliance

An intermediate small bank may also receive a rating of Needs to Improve or Substantial Noncompliance depending on the degree to which its performance has failed to meet the standards for a Satisfactory rating.

Lending Test for Small and Intermediate Small Banks

Satisfactory

The OCC rates a small or intermediate small bank's lending performance Satisfactory if, in general, the bank demonstrates

- A reasonable loan-to-deposit ratio (considering seasonal variations) given the bank's size, financial condition, the credit needs of its assessment area(s), and taking into account, as appropriate, other lending-related activities such as loan originations for sale to the secondary markets and community development loans and qualified investments;
- A majority of its loans and, as appropriate, other lending-related activities are in its assessment area(s);
- A distribution of loans to and, as appropriate, other lending-related activities for individuals of different income levels (including low- and moderate-income individuals) and businesses and farms of different sizes that is reasonable given the demographics of the bank's assessment area(s);
- A record of taking appropriate action, when warranted, in response to written complaints, if any, about the bank's performance in helping to meet the credit needs of its assessment area(s); and
- A reasonable geographic distribution of loans given the bank's assessment area(s).

Outstanding

A small or intermediate small bank that meets each of the standards for a Satisfactory rating and exceeds some or all of those standards may warrant consideration for a lending test rating of Outstanding.

Needs to Improve or Substantial Noncompliance

A small or intermediate small bank may receive a lending test rating of Needs to Improve or Substantial Noncompliance depending on the degree to which its performance has failed to meet the standards for a Satisfactory rating.

Community Development Test for Intermediate Small Banks

Satisfactory

The OCC rates an intermediate small bank's community development performance Satisfactory if the bank demonstrates adequate responsiveness to the community development needs of its assessment area(s) through community development loans, qualified investments, and community development services. The adequacy of the bank's response will depend on its capacity for such community development activities, its assessment area's need for such community development activities, and the availability of such opportunities for community development in the bank's assessment area(s).

Outstanding

The OCC rates an intermediate small bank's community development performance Outstanding if the bank demonstrates excellent responsiveness to community development needs in its assessment area(s) through community development loans, qualified investments, and community development services, as appropriate, considering the bank's capacity and the need and availability of such opportunities for community development in the bank's assessment area(s).

Needs to Improve or Substantial Noncompliance

An intermediate small bank may also receive a community development test rating of Needs to Improve or Substantial Noncompliance depending on the degree to which its performance has failed to meet the standards for a Satisfactory rating.

Strategic Plan Assessment and Rating

Satisfactory Goals

The OCC approves as Satisfactory, measurable goals that adequately help to meet the credit needs of the bank's assessment area(s).

Outstanding Goals

If the plan identifies a separate group of measurable goals that substantially exceed the levels approved as Satisfactory, the OCC will approve those goals as Outstanding.

The OCC assesses the performance of a bank operating under an approved plan to determine whether the bank has met its plan goals:

- If the bank substantially achieves its plan's goals for a Satisfactory rating, the OCC will rate the bank's performance under the plan as Satisfactory.

- If the bank exceeds its plan goals for a Satisfactory rating and substantially achieves its goals for an Outstanding rating, the OCC will rate the bank's performance as Outstanding.

- If the bank fails to meet substantially its plan goals for a satisfactory rating, the OCC will rate the bank as either Needs to Improve or Substantial Noncompliance, depending on the extent to which it falls short of its plan goals, unless the bank elected in its plan to be rated otherwise, as provided in 12 CFR 25.27(f)(4).

Appendix F: ROCA Rating System

ROCA, a management information and supervisory tool, rates the condition of a foreign banking organization's (FBO) branch or agency and systematically identifies significant supervisory concerns at the branch or agency. ROCA stands for Risk management, Operational controls, Compliance, and Asset quality. For evaluation purposes, the rating system divides a branch's or agency's overall activities into three components: risk management, operational controls, and compliance. These components represent the major activities or processes of a branch or agency that may raise supervisory concern. The system also rates the quality of the branch's or agency's stock of assets as of the examination date.

ROCA replaced the rating system known as AIM (Asset quality, Internal controls, and Management) because it better assesses the condition of a branch as part of an FBO. ROCA is also better at pinpointing the key areas of supervisory concern in a branch or agency office.

The OCC considers Bank Secrecy Act/anti-money laundering (BSA/AML) examination findings in a safety and soundness context when assigning the risk management component rating. Serious deficiencies in a branch's or agency's BSA/AML compliance create a presumption that the branch's or agency's risk management rating will be adversely affected because risk management practices are less than satisfactory. Examiners also consider BSA/AML examination findings when assigning the compliance component rating. Examiners should document application of this approach in their written comments in the OCC's supervisory information systems, and in supervisory communications, when appropriate. (Updated 9/28/2012)

Composite Rating

The overall or composite rating indicates whether, in the aggregate, the operations of the branch or agency may present supervisory concerns and the extent of any concerns. The composite rating should not be merely an arithmetic average of the component ratings; some components will often carry more weight than others. (For example, asset quality will carry more weight as the financial strength of the FBO weakens.) The examiner should assign and justify in the report a composite rating using the definitions provided below as a guide.

The composite rating is based on a scale from 1 (the least supervisory concern) through 5 (the most supervisory concern). The five composite ratings are defined as follows:

Composite Rating 1—Branches and agencies in this group are strong in every respect. These branches and agencies require only normal supervisory attention.

Composite Rating 2—Branches and agencies in this group are in satisfactory condition, but may have modest weaknesses that can be corrected by the branch's or agency's management in the normal course of business. Generally, they do not require additional or more than normal supervisory attention.

Composite Rating 3—Branches and agencies in this group are in fair condition because of a combination of weaknesses in risk management, operational controls, and compliance, or asset quality problems that, in combination with the condition of the FBO or other factors, cause supervisory concern. In addition, the branch's or agency's management or head office management may not be taking the necessary corrective actions to address substantive weaknesses. This rating may also be assigned when risk management, operational controls, or compliance is individually viewed as unsatisfactory. Generally, these branches and agencies raise supervisory concern and require more than normal supervisory attention to address their weaknesses.

Composite Rating 4—Branches and agencies in this group are in marginal condition because of serious weaknesses as reflected in the assessments of the individual components. Serious problems or unsafe and unsound banking practices or operations exist, which have not been satisfactorily addressed or resolved by the branch's or agency's management and/or head office management. Branches and agencies in this category require close supervisory attention and surveillance monitoring, as well as a definitive plan for corrective action by the branch's or agency's management and head office management.

Composite Rating 5—Branches and agencies in this group are in unsatisfactory condition because of a high level of severe weaknesses or unsafe and unsound conditions and consequently require urgent restructuring of operations by the branch's or agency's management and head office management.

Disclosure

Following approval of the rating by appropriate senior supervisory officials at the examining agency, the composite and component numeric ratings should be disclosed in the "Examination Conclusions and Comments" section of the examination report. When the rating is disclosed, its meaning should be explained clearly using the appropriate composite and component rating definitions. The report should also make it clear that, as part of the overall findings of the examination, the rating is confidential.

Component Evaluations

Like the composite rating, the component ratings are evaluated on a scale from 1 to 5, 1 representing the lowest level of supervisory concern and 5 representing the highest. Each component is discussed below followed by a description of the individual performance ratings.

Risk Management

Every financial institution is exposed to risk. Risk management, or the process of identifying, measuring, and controlling risk, is an important responsibility of any financial institution. A branch or agency is typically removed from its head office by location and time zone; therefore, an effective risk management system is critical not only to manage the scope of its activities but to achieve comprehensive, ongoing oversight by local and head office management. Examiners should determine the extent to which risk management techniques enable local and head office management (1) to achieve and maintain oversight of the branch's or agency's activities and (2) to control risk exposures that result from the branch's or agency's activities.

The primary components of a sound risk management system are a comprehensive risk assessment approach; a detailed structure of limits and other guidelines that govern risk taking; and a strong management information system for monitoring and reporting risks.

In assessing risks, the branch or agency identifies each risk associated with its activities (both on and off the balance sheet) and groups them into risk categories. These categories broadly relate to credit, market, liquidity, operational, and legal risks.[54] All major risks should be measured explicitly and consistently by branch management, and they should be reevaluated on an ongoing basis as economic circumstances, market conditions, and the branch's or agency's activities change. The branch's or agency's expansion into new products or business lines should not outpace proper risk management or the head office's supervision. When risks cannot be explicitly measured, management should demonstrate knowledge of their potential impact and an ability to manage them.

Risk identification and measurement are followed by an evaluation of risks and returns to establish acceptable risk exposure levels. The branch's or agency's lending and trading policies establish these levels, subject to the approval of head office management. Policies should set standards for undertaking and evaluating risk exposure in individual branch or agency activities as well as procedures for tracking and reporting risk exposure to monitor compliance with established policy limits or guidelines.

Head office management has a role in developing and approving the branch's risk management system as part of its responsibility to provide a comprehensive system of oversight for the branch or agency. Generally, the branch's or agency's risk management system, including risk identification, measurement, limits or guidelines, and monitoring, should be modeled on that of the FBO. Doing so ensures a fully integrated, organization-wide risk management system.

In assigning the risk management rating, examiners should evaluate the branch's or agency's current situation, concentrating on developments since the previous examination. The rating should not concentrate on past problems, such as those relating to the current quality of the branch's or agency's stock of assets, if risk management techniques have improved significantly since those problems developed.[55]

---

[54] While operational risks are identified in the branch's or agency's overall risk assessment, the effectiveness of the branch's or agency's operational controls is evaluated separately.

[55] Thus, for example, the change in the level of problem assets since the previous examination would normally be more important than the absolute level of problem assets. At the same time, a loan portfolio that has few borrowers experiencing debt service problems does not necessarily indicate a sound risk management system because underwriting standards may make the branch vulnerable to credit problems during a future economic downturn.

A **rating of 1** indicates that management has implemented a fully integrated risk management system. The system effectively identifies and controls all major types of risk at the branch or agency, including those from new products and the changing environment. This assessment, in most cases, will be supported by a superior level of financial performance and asset quality at the branch or agency. No supervisory concerns are evident.

A **rating of 2** indicates that the risk management system is fully effective with respect to almost all major risk factors. It reflects a responsiveness and ability to cope successfully with existing and foreseeable exposures that may arise in carrying out the branch's or agency's business plan. While the branch or agency may have residual weaknesses from past exposures, its management or the head office's management is addressing these problems. Any such weaknesses will not have a material adverse effect on the branch or agency. Generally, risks are being controlled in a manner that does not require additional or greater-than-normal supervisory attention.

A **rating of 3** signifies a risk management system that is lacking in some important respects. Its relative ineffectiveness in dealing with the branch's or agency's risk exposures is cause for greater-than-normal supervisory attention, and deterioration in financial performance indicators is probable. Current risk-related procedures are considered fair, existing problems are not being satisfactorily addressed, or risks are not being adequately identified and controlled. While these deficiencies may not have caused significant problems yet, there are clear indications that the branch or agency is vulnerable to risk-related deterioration.

A **rating of 4** indicates a marginal risk management system that generally fails to identify and control significant risk exposures in many important respects. Generally, such circumstances reflect a lack of adequate guidance and supervision by head office management. As a result, deterioration in overall performance is imminent or is already evident in the branch's or agency's overall performance since the previous examination. Failure of management to correct risk management deficiencies that have created significant problems in the past warrants close supervisory attention.

A **rating of 5** indicates that the branch or agency has critical performance problems that are due to the absence of an effective risk management system in almost every respect. Not only is there a large volume of problem risk exposures but the problems are also intensifying. Management has not demonstrated the ability to stabilize the branch's or agency's situation. If corrective actions are not taken immediately, the branch's or agency's ability to continue operating is in jeopardy.

Operational Controls

This component assesses the effectiveness of the branch's or agency's operational controls, including accounting and financial controls. Examiners expect branches and agencies to have an independent internal audit function, an adequate system of head office or external audits, or both. They should have a system of internal controls consistent with the size and complexity of their operations. Internal audit and control procedures should ensure that operations are conducted in accordance with internal guidelines and regulatory policies and that all reports and analyses provided to the head office and branch or agency senior management are comprehensive, timely, and accurate.

The OCC's supervision of a branch's or agency's operational controls has two basic goals. The first goal is to prevent branches and agencies participating in U.S. financial markets from undermining the high standards, efficiency, and confidence in the U.S. markets. The second goal is to ensure that head office management has adequate internal controls in place at the branch or agency (1) to ensure that the branch or agency is operating within corporate policies, and (2) to enable head office management, as well as the home country supervisor, to supervise the FBO on a consolidated basis in accordance with the supervisory principles of the Basel Committee on Banking Supervision.

A **rating of 1** indicates that the branch or agency has a fully comprehensive system of operational controls that protects against losses from transactional and operational risks and ensures accurate financial reporting. In addition, branch or agency operations are fully consistent with sound market practices. The branch or agency also has a well-defined and independent audit function that is appropriate to the size and risk profile of the branch or agency. No supervisory concerns are evident.

A **rating of 2** may indicate some minor weaknesses, such as modest control deficiencies caused by new business activities, that management is addressing. Some recommendations may be noted. Overall, the system of controls, including the audit function, is considered satisfactory and effective in maintaining a safe and sound branch or agency operation. Only routine supervisory attention is required.

A **rating of 3** indicates that the branch's or agency's system of controls, including the quality of the audit function, is lacking in some important respects. Particular weakness is evidenced by continued control exceptions, substantial deficiencies in written policies and procedures, or the failure to adhere to written policies and procedures. As a result, greater-than-normal supervisory attention is required.

A **rating of 4** signifies that the branch's or agency's system of operational controls has serious deficiencies that require substantial improvement. In such a case, the branch or agency may lack control functions, including those related to the audit function, that meet minimal expectations. Therefore, the branch's or agency's adherence to FBO and regulatory policies is questionable. Head office management has failed to give the branch or agency proper support to maintain operations in accordance with U.S. norms. Close supervisory attention is required.

A **rating of 5** indicates that the branch's or agency's system of operational controls is so inadequate that its operations are in serious jeopardy. The branch or agency either lacks an audit function or has a wholly deficient one. The branch's or agency's management should improve operational controls immediately. Examiners should give the situation strong supervisory attention.

Compliance

Branches and agencies should demonstrate compliance with all applicable state and federal laws and regulations, including reporting and special supervisory requirements. To the extent possible, given the size and risk profile of the branch or agency, these responsibilities should be vested in a branch or agency official or compliance officer who is not a line manager and does not report to one. Branch or agency management should regularly ensure that all appropriate personnel are properly trained in meeting regulatory requirements. The audit function should be sufficient in scope to ensure that the branch or agency is meeting all applicable regulatory requirements.

A **rating of 1** indicates an outstanding level of compliance with applicable laws, regulations, and reporting requirements. No supervisory concerns are evident.

A **rating of 2** indicates that compliance is generally effective with respect to most factors. Compliance monitoring and related training programs are sufficient to prevent significant problems. Although minor reporting errors may be present, they are being adequately addressed by branch or agency management. Only normal supervisory attention is warranted.

A **rating of 3** indicates that deficiencies in management and training systems have produced an atmosphere in which significant compliance problems could and do occur. Such deficiencies could include the lack of written compliance procedures, the absence of a system for identifying possible compliance issues, or a substantial number of minor or repeat violations or deficiencies. Greater-than-normal supervisory attention is warranted.

A **rating of 4** indicates that the branch's or agency's and head office's management does not give compliance matters proper attention. Close supervisory attention is warranted. The branch or agency may not have an effective compliance program or an ongoing training program. It may fail to meet significant regulatory requirements, or its regulatory reports may contain significant, widespread inaccuracies.

A **rating of 5** signals that the branch's or agency's attention to compliance matters is wholly lacking. Immediate supervisory attention is warranted.

Asset Quality

A national bank's asset quality is evaluated to determine whether it has sufficient capital to absorb prospective losses and, ultimately, whether it can maintain its viability as an ongoing enterprise. The evaluation of asset quality in a branch or agency does not have the same purpose because a branch or agency is not a separately capitalized entity. Instead, a branch's or agency's viability depends on the financial and managerial support of the FBO.

The ability of a branch or agency to honor its liabilities ultimately is based upon the FBO's condition and level of support from the FBO, *a concept that is integral to the FBO Supervision Program.* As indicated above, a branch or agency is not strictly limited by its own internal and external funding sources in meeting solvency and liquidity needs.

Nonetheless, the evaluation of asset quality is important in assessing both the effectiveness of credit risk management and the ability of the branch's or agency's assets to pay liabilities and claims in liquidation. (*Generally, credit administration concerns should be addressed in rating the risk management component.*)

In the OCC's FBO Supervision Program, an FBO whose financial condition is satisfactory is presumed to be able to support the branch or agency with sufficient capital and reserves on a consolidated basis. As a result, the assessment of asset quality in such circumstances would not be a predominant factor in the branch's or agency's overall assessment, if existing risk management techniques are satisfactory. If, however, the condition of the FBO is less than satisfactory and/or support from the FBO is questionable, the evaluation of asset quality should be carefully considered in determining whether supervisory actions are needed to improve the branch's or agency's ability to meet its obligations on a stand-alone basis. When a branch or agency is subject to asset maintenance, it is expected to address asset quality issues by removing classified assets from the list of eligible assets.

It may be appropriate for examiners to give the component for asset quality greater or lesser weight in a composite rating as the FBO's condition changes. For example, if the financial strength of the FBO weakens, the quality of assets booked in the United States becomes increasingly important as the source of protection for local creditors, and the "A" in ROCA should gain weight. Examiners may also choose to give the asset quality component more weight if the FBO's support for the branch or agency becomes questionable. But examiners should use their judgment in such circumstances. For example, a branch or agency that holds problem assets for other offices so that the FBO can better manage the workout process should not be penalized, so long as the FBO has the ability to support the level of problem assets. And when the FBO is strong and the need to look to local assets for protection of creditors seems remote, the quality of local assets is less important, and the "A" in ROCA should carry less weight.

A branch or agency accorded a **rating of 1** has strong asset quality.

A branch or agency accorded a **rating of 2** has satisfactory asset quality.

A branch or agency accorded a **rating of 3** has fair asset quality.

A branch or agency accorded a **rating of 4** has marginal asset quality.

A branch or agency accorded a **rating of 5** has unsatisfactory asset quality.

Appendix G: Disclosure of Ratings

Disclosing ratings to a bank's board of directors and senior management strengthens communications by encouraging more complete and open discussions of examination findings, conclusions, and recommendations. Using the information disclosed, bank management can better focus on possible areas of weaknesses and timely corrective measures.

Discussions with Senior Management

By longstanding policy, OCC examiners thoroughly discuss examination findings and conclusions during exit meetings with senior management or the board of directors, as appropriate. They discuss a bank's overall condition and its recommended composite rating, as well as conclusions about component areas. Since the January 1, 1997 implementation of the revised UFIRS, examiners have also disclosed the numeric ratings for all component areas.

During exit meetings, examiners discuss factors considered in assigning each component rating, as well as the overall composite rating. Discussions should indicate that the composite rating is based on a careful evaluation of a bank's managerial, operational, financial, and compliance performance. The composite rating assigned is not an arithmetic average of the component ratings but is based on a qualitative analysis of the factors comprising each component, the interrelationship between components, and the overall level of supervisory concern about the bank.

The quality of management is the single most important element in the successful operation of a national bank, and is usually the factor that is most indicative of how well risk is identified, measured, monitored, and controlled. For this reason, sufficient time should be taken to review and explain the factors considered when assigning a management component rating and the meaning of the assigned rating.

Discussion should indicate whether the ratings are preliminary or final.[56] If the ratings are preliminary, examiners should indicate that final composite and component ratings will be assigned by the bank's supervisory office. Final ratings will be disclosed, as appropriate, in the written report of examination or the transmittal letter that is submitted to the bank.

Finally, management should be informed that, except for the Community Reinvestment Act assessment, composite and component ratings disclosed in the report of examination or other written communication remain subject to the confidentiality rules imposed by 12 CFR 4.[57]

---

[56] For CRA examinations, examiners will disclose the preliminary rating to bank management prior to completing the examination, but only after obtaining supervisory office concurrence.

[57] Each ROE must contain a confidentiality disclosure statement alerting readers that the entire ROE is confidential, including composite and component ratings. Refer to appendix I for more information on ROE content, structure, and review requirements.

Reports of Examination

Comments on the Examination Conclusions and Comments page and other appropriate pages in the report should fully support the component and composite ratings assigned. When used, individual core pages of the report should contain information that is clear, informative, and appropriate in tone, and that explains the findings and conclusions that support the assigned ratings.

Consolidated Reports

The numeric CAMELS composite rating, the CAMELS component ratings, and the information technology, trust, and consumer compliance ratings (collectively known as CAMELS/ITC) are disclosed at the top of the Examination Conclusions and Comments page of the report of examination. The CRA rating may also be disclosed here. What follows is an example of how examiners should disclose ratings on this page.

	Current Rating	Current Rating Date	Prior Rating	Prior Rating Date
Composite Uniform Financial Institution Rating	2	xx/xx/xxxx	2	xx/xx/xxxx
Component Ratings:				
Capital Adequacy	2	xx/xx/xxxx	2	xx/xx/xxxx
Asset Quality	2	xx/xx/xxxx	2	xx/xx/xxxx
Management	2	xx/xx/xxxx	2	xx/xx/xxxx
Earnings	2	xx/xx/xxxx	2	xx/xx/xxxx
Liquidity	2	xx/xx/xxxx	2	xx/xx/xxxx
Sensitivity to Market Risk	2	xx/xx/xxxx	2	xx/xx/xxxx
Information Technology	2	xx/xx/xxxx	2	xx/xx/xxxx
Trust	2	xx/xx/xxxx	2	xx/xx/xxxx
Consumer Compliance	2	xx/xx/xxxx	2	xx/xx/xxxx
Community Reinvestment Act	Satisfactory	xx/xx/xxxx	Satisfactory	xx/xx/xxxx

Narrative CAMELS/ITC pages also show the individual numeric rating for the area being discussed. The individual numeric rating is shown in a line immediately following the descriptive heading on each page (e.g., Component Rating 2). The descriptive headings at the top of the narrative CAMELS/ITC pages reflect the evaluation factors associated with the areas.

For CRA findings and conclusions that have been included in a consolidated or concurrent examination report, the performance rating should be disclosed on the Examination Conclusions and Comments page with a statement that the reader should refer to the public evaluation for details and applicable component and sub-ratings.

For federal branch and agency examinations, ROCA composite and component (risk management, operational controls, compliance, and asset quality) ratings are disclosed in examination reports in a manner similar to commercial examinations.

Stand-Alone Specialty Reports

Findings and conclusions of specialty area examinations may be presented in a separate stand-alone examination report. If so, the format for disclosing these ratings should be similar to the format for a consolidated or concurrent examination report with disclosure of ratings on the Examination Conclusions and Comments page.

When a stand-alone IT report is issued for a bank that provides technology services to other financial institutions, the bank's IT rating should be disclosed in an accompanying transmittal letter in order to prevent disclosure to serviced financial institutions that may receive copies of the report.

Appendix H: Categories of Risk

For supervision purposes, the OCC has defined eight categories of risk to a bank's earnings, capital, or franchise or enterprise value. These categories are not mutually exclusive. Any product or service may expose a bank to multiple risks. Risks also may be interdependent and may be positively or negatively correlated. Examiners should be aware of this interdependence and assess the effect in a consistent and inclusive manner. (Updated 5/06/2013)

Credit Risk

Credit risk is the risk to current or anticipated earnings or capital arising from an obligor's failure to meet the terms of any contract with the bank or otherwise perform as agreed. Credit risk is found in all activities in which settlement or repayment depends on counterparty, issuer, or borrower performance. It exists any time bank funds are extended, committed, invested, or otherwise exposed through actual or implied contractual agreements, whether reflected on or off the balance sheet. (Updated 5/06/2013)

Credit risk is the most recognizable risk associated with banking. This definition, however, encompasses more than the traditional definition associated with lending activities. Credit risk also arises in conjunction with a broad range of bank activities, including selecting investment portfolio products, derivatives trading partners, or foreign exchange counterparties. Credit risk also arises due to country or sovereign exposure, as well as indirectly through guarantor performance. (Updated 5/06/2013)

Interest Rate Risk

Interest rate risk is the risk to current or anticipated earnings or capital arising from movements in interest rates. Interest rate risk results from differences between the timing of rate changes and the timing of cash flows (repricing risk); from changing rate relationships among different yield curves affecting bank activities (basis risk); from changing rate relationships across the spectrum of maturities (yield curve risk); and from interest-related options embedded in bank products (options risk). (Updated 5/06/2013)

The assessment of interest rate risk should consider risk from both an accounting perspective (i.e., the effect on the bank's accrual earnings) and an economic perspective (i.e., the effect on the market value of the bank's portfolio equity). In some banks, interest rate risk is included in the broader category of market risk. In contrast with price risk, which focuses on the mark-to-market portfolios (e.g., trading accounts), interest rate risk focuses on the value implications for accrual portfolios (e.g., held-to-maturity and available-for-sale accounts). (Updated 5/06/2013)

Liquidity Risk

Liquidity risk is the risk to current or anticipated earnings or capital arising from an inability to meet obligations when they come due. Liquidity risk includes the inability to access funding sources or manage fluctuations in funding levels. Liquidity risk also results from a bank's failure to recognize or address changes in market conditions that affect its ability to liquidate assets quickly and with minimal loss in value. (Updated 5/06/2013)

Liquidity risk, like credit risk, is a recognizable risk associated with banking. The nature of liquidity risk, however, has changed in recent years. Increased investment alternatives for retail depositors, sophisticated off-balance-sheet products with complicated cash-flow implications, and a general increase in the credit sensitivity of bank customers are all examples of factors that complicate liquidity risk. (Updated 5/06/2013)

Price Risk

Price risk is the risk to current or anticipated earnings or capital arising from changes in the value of either trading portfolios or other obligations that are entered into as part of distributing risk. These portfolios typically are subject to daily price movements and are accounted for primarily on a mark-to-market basis. This risk occurs most significantly from market-making, dealing, and position-taking in interest rate, foreign exchange, equity, commodities, and credit markets. (Updated 5/06/2013)

Price risk also arises from bank activities whose value changes are reflected in the income statement, such as in lending pipelines, other real estate owned, and mortgage servicing rights. The risk to earnings or capital resulting from the conversion of a bank's financial statements from foreign currency translation also should be assessed under price risk. As with interest rate risk, many banks include price risk in the broader category of market risk. (Updated 5/06/2013)

Operational Risk

Operational risk is the risk to current or anticipated earnings or capital arising from inadequate or failed internal processes or systems, human errors or misconduct, or adverse external events. Operational losses result from internal fraud; external fraud; inadequate or inappropriate employment practices and workplace safety; failure to meet professional obligations involving clients, products, and business practices; damage to physical assets; business disruption and systems failures; and failures in execution, delivery, and process management. Operational losses do not include opportunity costs, forgone revenue, or costs related to risk management and control enhancements implemented to prevent future operational losses. (Updated 5/06/2013)

The quantity of operational risk and the quality of operational risk management are heavily influenced by the quality and effectiveness of a bank's system of internal control. The quality of the audit function, although independent of operational risk management, also is a key assessment factor. Audit can affect the operating performance of a bank by helping to identify and ensure correction of weaknesses in risk management or controls. The quality of due diligence and business continuity planning are other key assessment factors for mitigating operational risk arising from third-party relationships and events outside a bank's direct control, such as natural disasters and damage to or loss of critical infrastructure. (Updated 5/06/2013)

Compliance Risk

Compliance risk is the risk to current or anticipated earnings or capital arising from violations of laws, rules, or regulations, or from nonconformance with prescribed practices, internal policies and procedures, or ethical standards. This risk exposes a bank to fines, civil money penalties, payment of damages, and the voiding of contracts. Compliance risk can result in diminished reputation, reduced franchise or enterprise value, limited business opportunities, and lessened expansion potential. (Updated 5/06/2013)

Compliance risk is not limited to risk from failure to comply with consumer protection laws; it encompasses the risk of noncompliance with *all* laws and regulations, as well as prudent ethical standards and contractual obligations. It also includes the exposure to litigation (known as legal risk) from all aspects of banking, traditional and nontraditional. (Updated 5/06/2013)

Strategic Risk

Strategic risk is the risk to current or anticipated earnings, capital, or franchise or enterprise value arising from adverse business decisions, poor implementation of business decisions, or lack of responsiveness to changes in the banking industry and operating environment. This risk is a function of a bank's strategic goals, business strategies, resources, and quality of implementation. The resources needed to carry out business strategies are both tangible and intangible. They include communication channels, operating systems, delivery networks, and managerial capacities and capabilities. (Updated 5/06/2013)

The assessment of strategic risk includes more than an analysis of a bank's written strategic plan. It focuses on opportunity costs and how plans, systems, and implementation affect the bank's franchise or enterprise value. It also incorporates how management analyzes external factors, such as economic, technological, competitive, regulatory, and other environmental changes, that affect the bank's strategic direction. (Updated 5/06/2013)

Reputation Risk

Reputation risk is the risk to current or anticipated earnings, capital, or franchise or enterprise value arising from negative public opinion. This risk may impair a bank's competitiveness by affecting its ability to establish new relationships or services or continue servicing existing relationships. Reputation risk is inherent in all bank activities and requires management to exercise an abundance of caution in dealing with customers, counterparties, correspondents, investors, and the community. (Updated 5/06/2013)

A bank that actively associates its name with products and services offered through outsourced arrangements or asset management affiliates is more likely to have higher reputation risk exposure. Significant threats to a bank's reputation also may result from negative publicity regarding matters such as unethical or deceptive business practices, violations of laws or regulations, high-profile litigation, or poor financial performance. The assessment of reputation risk should take into account the bank's culture, the effectiveness of its problem-escalation processes and rapid-response plans, and its deployment of media. (Updated 5/06/2013)

Appendix I: ROE Content, Structure, and Review Requirements

Since 1993, the OCC has used the interagency uniform common core ROE format.[58] More recently, the federal banking agencies agreed to a flexible approach in using this format for examination reports.

In community and mid-size national banks, a streamlined ROE is used in banks that have composite ratings of 1 or 2. **A streamlined ROE must contain the mandatory items listed in appendix C of the "Community Bank Supervision" booklet, either as individual ROE pages or as part of the Examination Conclusions and Comments page.** Examiners should include supplemental pages, as appropriate, based on the risk profile of the bank and the results of the supervisory activities. If any component rating is 3 or worse, the examiner must use the appropriate narrative page. Other schedules related to that component rating should also be used, as needed. In addition, the examiner will use the appropriate narrative page to communicate significant supervisory concerns, such as unwarranted risk taking. A narrative page can also be used to explain why supervisory activities were expanded for a bank having a high overall risk profile.[59]

The uniform common core ROE is still required for

- Banks with composite ratings of 3 or worse, or
- Community banks that have been in operation less than 3 years.

In large banks, the ROE is usually a summary of examiners' conclusions about the bank's condition drawn from the results of supervisory activities throughout the 12-month cycle. Examiners should use the uniform common core ROE for banks with total assets of $1 billion or more. Exceptions are permitted when other communications with the bank clearly communicate the institution's composite and component CAMELS ratings and delineate the significant risks. When copies of alternative communications are provided to other financial institution regulators or functional regulators, examiners should ensure that the correspondence is sufficiently informative to convey the bank's condition and enable those regulators to reach similar conclusions. The OCC does not require use of the common core ROE for smaller affiliated national banks of a multibank organization. Regardless of the format, communications with affiliated banks must disclose significant findings, the adequacy of the bank's BSA compliance program, the affiliate's condition, and the composite and component CAMELS ratings.[60]

In federal branches and agencies, examiners use a modified uniform common core ROE. The ROE details the results of the examination while assessing the branch's role within the consolidated company. The ROE is sent to the federal branch or agency. It cannot be sent to the head office. Although the branch or agency may share the information with its head

---

[58] Refer to Examining Bulletin 93-7, "Interagency Common Core Report of Examination."
[59] The "Community Bank Supervision" booklet has further guidance on streamlined ROEs.
[60] For additional guidance on written communication in large and mid-size banks and their smaller national bank affiliates, refer to the "Large Bank Supervision" booklet.

office, the OCC cannot be assured that an ROE sent to a head office will be adequately protected from disclosure (because the laws governing confidentiality and customer privacy differ from nation to nation). A letter is sent annually to the parent entity's board and home country supervisor summarizing the foreign bank's U.S. federal operations. In the event problems are discovered during the course of an examination, the examiner may contact head office management to solicit its support for correcting deficiencies.

Findings from targeted examinations of areas such as compliance or a credit product may be communicated in a separate written supervisory communication or incorporated into the ROE at the end of the supervisory cycle using the appropriate optional page. If separate communications are sent for targeted examinations, the supervisory cycle ROE should reference the communications and summarize any significant findings.

The ROE or written supervisory communication shall address the overall adequacy of the bank's BSA compliance program, including a description of any problems as required by 12 USC 1818(s)(2)(B). In formulating a written conclusion, the examiner does not need to discuss every procedure performed during the examination.

Uniform Common Core ROE

The uniform common core report of examination consists of three sections: Mandatory Core pages, Optional Core pages, and Supplemental pages.

Mandatory Core pages are required in each report where a uniform common core ROE is required. Besides the cover page, table of contents, and Signatures of Directors page, the Mandatory Core pages are Examination Conclusions and Comments, Matters Requiring Attention, CAMELS Narratives, Risk Assessment Summary, and Schedules. Financial information and ratios cannot be deleted from these pages, but additional data to support conclusions may be included in the narrative portion of any page.

The EIC may use Optional Core pages to further support examination findings. These pages must be used as formatted if they are included in the report. Optional Core pages must follow the Mandatory Core pages, although the Signatures of Directors page is always the final page in the ROE.

The EIC may use Supplemental pages to support Mandatory Core page analysis. There is no prescribed format for these pages, and they can be interspersed among Optional Core pages. They cannot be interspersed among Mandatory Core pages.

Optional Core pages and Supplemental pages should be included in the report only if they are necessary to address supervisory activities pertinent to the bank or to support examination conclusions.

Mandatory Core Pages

<u>Cover Page</u>

The cover page identifies the bank and the examination discussed in the report. Other information required on this page includes the

- Location of the bank—include city and state as a minimum.
- Charter number of the bank.
- Examination start date; i.e., the date examiners began work in the bank or began reviewing data for the examination.
- Correspondence address paragraph. (Examiners should select the paragraph referencing the supervisory office for the bank.)

<u>Table of Contents</u>

The table of contents provides an overview of report sections and pages. It helps the board locate information easily within the report. If the table of contents differs at all from one report to another, the reason will be the inclusion of different Optional Core pages or Supplemental pages.

<u>Examination Conclusions and Comments</u>

This page summarizes the significant findings of examination activities performed during the supervisory cycle, both positive and negative. It focuses the board's attention on excessive risks or significant deficiencies in risk management and their root causes, consistent with the objectives of the examination. Comments should be written using short narratives with bullet points when possible.

Examination objectives must be clearly stated and describe the purpose of the report. Objectives should be stated from the bank's perspective and should explain how the OCC's examination scope and activities during the supervisory cycle were used to evaluate the bank's overall condition.

Major conclusions and significant concerns, if any, are prioritized and summarized here along with a brief discussion of each CAMELS component and specialty area reviewed. Comments should provide the board a concise, unambiguous assessment of the overall condition of the bank. Comments should cross-reference other sections of the report containing greater detail, if necessary.

The bank's assigned composite, component, and specialty area ratings are disclosed on this page. The applicable composite rating definition can be included on this page, or on a Supplemental page if referenced here.[61]

---

[61] Refer to appendix G for additional guidance on disclosure of ratings.

This page will also include a summary of actions the institution should take in response to the OCC's supervisory findings, and the commitment to those actions made by the board and management during the examination. If no supervisory concerns are noted, the comment should so indicate; otherwise, clear direction should be provided for the board.

A brief discussion of any planned OCC follow-up should be included, such as

- Items/concerns remaining after exit meetings conducted with management during the examination.
- Plans for future board meetings.
- Requests for written responses from the board.
- The timing and content of progress reports.
- Expected timing/focus of future supervisory activities.
- Additional information to help the board understand the report, including
  - Persons to contact with questions or comments.
  - Notification that an enforcement action is being recommended for initiation or termination, or that a civil money penalty (CMP) referral is being considered or has been made. NOTE: Examiners should fully discuss enforcement actions and CMP referrals with the supervisory office or OCC legal counsel and receive concurrence before including them in the report.
  - Any other general information on the structure and content of the ROE.

A confidentiality disclosure statement must be included on this page or on the inside front cover of the ROE. The statement

- Alerts readers that the ROE is the property of the OCC and that its entire contents, including component and composite ratings, are strictly confidential.
- Details exceptions to the general prohibition on disclosure.
- Advises that the ROE is not an audit of the bank and does not relieve directors of their responsibility for performing or providing for adequate audits.
- Instructs directors to review and sign the ROE and informs them of what they should do if they are not in agreement with its contents and conclusions.

A signature block for the EIC and for the approving supervisory office official must be placed after the last paragraph of this comment. The EIC is not required to sign the report; typing his or her name and title will suffice. The report is not considered final until an approval authority signs it, either the supervisory office official or a person officially designated to act in that capacity.

Matters Requiring Attention

Matters Requiring Attention (MRA) are practices that

- Deviate from sound governance, internal control, and risk management principles, which may adversely impact the bank's earnings or capital, risk profile, or reputation, if not addressed; or

- Result in substantive noncompliance with laws and regulations, internal policies or processes, OCC supervisory guidance, or conditions imposed in writing in connection with the approval of any application or other request by a bank.[62]

This page focuses the board's attention on issues that require their immediate acknowledgement and oversight. Examiners should communicate these weaknesses to the board when discovered and should not defer listing them as MRAs pending bank management's efforts to address them. They should not employ a graduated process by first listing a practice meeting the MRA criteria as a recommendation,[63] then, if it is not addressed, as an MRA.

MRA comments should prioritize and further reflect concerns set forth in Examination Conclusions and Comments. Comments should be brief with reference(s) to supporting remarks elsewhere in the report. While there is no specific format for MRAs, examiners should

- Describe the MRA.
- Identify contributing factors or the root cause(s) of the MRA.
- Describe likely consequences or effects on the bank from inaction.
- Record management's commitment to corrective action.
- Include the time frame and the person(s) responsible for corrective action.

When discussing MRAs, examiners must be clear with management and the board of directors regarding our supervisory concerns and expectations. Examiners must impress upon the board its responsibility to ensure that management implements corrective actions within a reasonable period of time and to confirm that those actions are effective. Failure to do so could lead to enforcement actions. Therefore, banks should have a process for following up on MRAs. Likewise, examiners should include plans to follow up on MRAs in strategies for individual banks.

If there are no matters requiring attention, the word "None" must be inserted on this page.

CAMELS Narrative Pages

The report includes a page for each CAMELS component. These pages present support for overall conclusions discussed in Examination Conclusions and Comments and can detail items in Matters Requiring Attention.

Headings at the top of each CAMELS page identify factors related to evaluating that area. The narrative comment does not have to address all the factors listed in each page heading.

---

[62] Refer to "Conditions Imposed in Writing" for more information.

[63] Recommendations must be clearly distinguished from MRAs in the ROE. Recommendations can be included on applicable report pages as suggestions to enhance policies or as best practices. Recommendations do not require specific action by bank management or follow-up by examiners. Recommendations are not tracked in the OCC's supervisory information systems.

The examiner's comments should address only the factors having significant influence on an area's evaluation. Discussions related to other report comments may be cross-referenced. Ratios or comparisons to peer averages in report narratives can be helpful, but should be presented in proper perspective and thoroughly explained to ensure that the board and management do not misinterpret them.

Narrative comments can be used to explain significant variances in ratios/data between the examination "as of" date and its actual "start" date. This is particularly important if variances affect examination conclusions.

Risk Assessment Summary

This page contains examiners' assessments of the quantity of risk, quality of risk management, aggregate level of risk, and the direction of risk for each risk category using the risk assessment system (RAS) matrix. A brief narrative comment under the RAS matrix should be included for each risk category.

Schedule Pages

Other Mandatory Core pages include

- Concentrations of Credit.
- Summary of Items Subject to Adverse Classification/Summary of Items Listed as Special Mention.
- Comparative Statements of Financial Condition.
- Analysis of Earnings.

Examiners should refer to OCC Bulletin 95-7, "Concentrations of Credit," when preparing the Concentrations of Credit page. For concentrations that pose a challenge to management or present unusual or significant risk to the bank, comments should address, as necessary, the quality of concentrations management, appropriateness of risk limits, and the accuracy of reporting.

Financial data in the report will usually represent the most recent final quarterly data available from the Financial Institution Data Retrieval System (FINDRS). All financial schedules must be prepared as of the same date, which should normally be the examination "as of" date. A "review" date can be used to reflect certain data for the asset quality review, if it is different from the "as of" date.

An examiner may prepare the financial schedule pages using more current data than the data available from FINDRS. However, doing so will require manual calculation of the data using the definitions in *A User's Guide for the Uniform Bank Performance Report.*

Signatures of Directors

This page is used by members of the board of directors to document its review of the report. By signing this page, each director shows that he or she has personally reviewed the entire report.

In lieu of all board members signing the report, members of a committee may sign for the board if (1) the committee membership includes outside directors and (2) the full board has passed a resolution delegating review of the report to that committee. In such circumstances, the board members who do not sign are no less responsible for the safe and sound operation of the bank. The Signatures of Directors page will always be the last page of the report.

Optional Core Pages

The Optional Core pages are used to support examination conclusions, concerns, and recommendations as appropriate. They should not be used if a Mandatory page narrative can effectively support examination conclusions. Optional Core pages are formatted to provide additional information in the report, such as write-ups for assets adversely classified, credit data or collateral documentation exceptions, loans with structural weaknesses, and past due and nonaccrual loans and leases. Other Optional Core pages are available for narratives on other areas of examination interest, such as compliance with enforcement actions, violations of laws and regulations, specialty areas, and other matters.

When write-ups of violations of laws or regulations are included in the report, they should list and detail all violations in numerical sequence by legal type. Violations of United States Codes (USC) should be listed first, followed by violations of federal regulations (CFR), and then other violations. Write-ups of violations must

- Properly detail the legal numerical cites and name.
- Include a brief description of the law or regulation (or portion of it) that is in violation.
- Specify what led to the violation.
- Show the corrective action taken or promised by management.

The following information, as appropriate, may be included in the write-up:

- Dates of violations.
- Any dollar amounts involved.
- Duration of the violation.
- Approving directors.
- Recurring violations.
- Association with one individual or department of the bank.
- Whether acts leading to the violation appear intentional.
- Plans for restitution by responsible parties if the bank has suffered a loss.

Write-ups for assets subject to adverse classification should follow the guidelines in the "Rating Credit Risk" booklet of the *Comptroller's Handbook*.

Supplemental Pages

Examiners will use Supplemental pages to present supporting information not captured in other report pages. These pages are not preformatted.

For example, examination comments related to a bank's retail non-deposit investment products (i.e., mutual funds, annuities) could be included on a Supplemental page. The examiner could entitle the page "Retail Non-deposit Investment Products," make each product a subheading, and comment briefly on each product. If comments on any product are lengthy, the product should be featured on its own page.

The examiner may use any Optional Core Page or Supplemental Page. However, these pages should not be used if a Mandatory Core Page narrative can more effectively explain and support the examiner's conclusions.

Review and Processing

Before the ROE is completed, the EIC will provide drafts of the Examination Conclusions and Comments and Matters Requiring Attention pages to bank management so they may review them for accuracy. An appropriate OCC supervisory office official should review the examination findings before the drafts are provided to bank management.

Reports must be processed efficiently. They should clearly communicate results of supervisory activities and be distributed to all appropriate parties within established time frames.

Each district, mid-size, and large bank Deputy Comptroller should establish internal procedures and control systems to ensure that

- Supervisory offices prepare, review, and transmit reports and other written communication within a reasonable time after completion of an examination activity.

- Report preparers follow established standards for report quality.

- Examiners and supervisory offices assign accurate CAMELS composite and component ratings or specialty area ratings.

- The responsible approving supervisory office official signs the report.

- Report reviewers notify report preparers of any substantive modifications, errors, or omissions, and maintain documentation supporting their revisions.

- Districts or supervisory offices track and analyze report processing time frames and approve any extended time frames.

- Supervisory offices distribute reports to the following, as appropriate:
  - Bank.
  - Federal Reserve Bank district office.
  - FDIC regional office.
  - Field office.
  - District office.
  - Central Records at the Washington office.
  - National banks serviced by an information technology service provider rated 4 or 5 by OCC.

References

Laws

12 USC 481, "Appointment of Examiners; Examination of Member Banks, State Banks, and Trust Companies; Reports"

12 USC 1818(i)(2), "Civil Money Penalty"

12 USC 1818(s)(2), "Monetary Transaction Recordkeeping and Report Requirements Compliance Examinations"

12 USC 1820(d), "On-site Examinations of Insured Depository Institutions"

12 USC 1820(i)(1), "Flood Insurance Compliance Examinations"

12 USC 1841(c)(2)(D), "Trust Banks"

12 USC 1841(c)(2)(F), "CEBA Credit Card Banks"

12 USC 1867, "Regulation and Examination of Bank Service Companies"

12 USC 3105(c)(1), "Examination of Branches, Agencies, and Affiliates"

15 USC 78o-4(c)(7), "Examination of Municipal Securities Dealers"

15 USC 78o-5(d)(1), "Examination of Government Securities Dealers"

42 USC 4012a(f), "Civil Money Penalties for Failure to Require Flood Insurance or Notify"

"Federal Deposit Insurance Corporation Improvement Act of 1991" (FDICIA)

"Gramm-Leach-Bliley Act of 1999" (GLBA)

"Riegle Community Development and Regulatory Improvement Act of 1994" (CDRI)

Regulations

12 CFR 4.6, "Frequency of Examination of National Banks"

12 CFR 4.7, "Frequency of Examination of Federal Agencies and Branches"

12 CFR 6, "Prompt Corrective Action"

12 CFR 21—Subpart B, "Reports of Suspicious Activities"

12 CFR 21—Subpart C, "Procedures for Monitoring Bank Secrecy Act Compliance"

12 CFR 25, "Community Reinvestment Act"

12 CFR 30, "Safety and Soundness Standards"

Comptroller's Handbook

Comptroller's Handbook, "Asset Management"

Comptroller's Handbook, "Community Bank Supervision"

Comptroller's Handbook, "Consumer Compliance Examination"

Comptroller's Handbook, "Federal Branches and Agencies Supervision"

Comptroller's Handbook, "Internal and External Audits"

Comptroller's Handbook, "Internal Control"

Comptroller's Handbook, "Internal Control Questionnaires and Verification Procedures"

Comptroller's Handbook, "Large Bank Supervision"

Comptroller's Handbook, "Rating Credit Risk"

Comptroller's Licensing Manual, "Charters"

Comptroller's Licensing Manual, "Conversions"

OCC Issuances

Banking Bulletin 93-38, "Interagency Examination Coordination Guidelines"
Banking Circular 270, "Civil Money Penalty Assessment for Delinquent or Inaccurate Call Reports"
Banking Circular 273, "Civil Money Penalties"
Examining Bulletin 93-7, Interagency Common Core Report of Examination"
Guide to the Interagency Country Exposure Review Committee Process
OCC Bulletin 95-7, "Concentrations of Credit"
OCC Bulletin 2002-9, "National Bank Appeals Process"
OCC Bulletin 2002-38, "Enforcement Action Policy"
OCC Bulletin 2004-20, "Risk Management of New, Expanded, or Modified Bank Products and Services"
OCC Bulletin 2004-51, "Enforcement Action Policy"
OCC Bulletin 2007-21, "Supervision of National Trust Banks"
OCC Bulletin 2007-31, "Prohibition on Political Contributions by National Banks"
OCC Bulletin 2007-36, "Interagency Statement on Enforcement of Bank Secrecy Act/Anti-Money Laundering Requirements"
PPM 1000-9 (Revised), "Administering Appeals from National Banks"
PPM 1000-11, "Communications with Banks in the Examination Process"
PPM 5000-7 (Revised), "Civil Money Penalties"
PPM 5000-23, "Report Review and Processing"
PPM 5000-27 (Revised), "Civil Money Penalty Assessment for Delinquent or Inaccurate Call Reports"
PPM 5000-35, "Examiner View"
PPM 5000-38 (Revised), "Large Bank EIC Rotation"
PPM 5100-2 (Revised), "Shared National Credit Program"
PPM 5310-3 (Revised), "Enforcement Action Policy"
PPM 5310-3 (Revised), Supplement 1, "Enforcement Action Policy: Appendix C"
PPM 5310-8 (Revised), "Fast Track Enforcement Program"
PPM 5310-10, "Guidance to Examiners in Securing Access to Bank Books and Records"
PPM 5400-8 (Revised), "Supervision Work Papers"
PPM 5400-9 (Revised), "De Novo and Converted Banks"
PPM 5500-1 (Revised), "Coordination with Foreign Supervisors"
PPM 6000-5, "OCC Documents"
PPM 6100-3 (Revised), "Policies on Interagency Exchange of Supervisory Information and Coordination of Formal Corrective Action"
SIS-Examiner View Help
WISDM User's Guide

Other

Federal Register, Volume 61, No. 245, December 19, 1996, Pages 67021-67029, Uniform Financial Institutions Rating System

Federal Register, Volume 63, No. 197, October 13, 1998, Pages 54704-54711, Uniform Interagency Trust Rating System

Federal Register, Volume 64, No. 12, January 20, 1999, Pages 3109-3116, Uniform Rating System for Information Technology

Federal Reserve System, *Examination Manual for U.S. Branches and Agencies of Foreign Banking Organizations*

FFIEC, *Bank Secrecy Act/Anti-Money Laundering Examination Manual*

FFIEC, *Information Technology Examination Handbook*

FFIEC, *A User's Guide for the Uniform Bank Performance Report*

MSRB, Rule G-16

www.ingramcontent.com/pod-product-compliance
Lightning Source LLC
Chambersburg PA
CBHW080304290526
45790CB00005B/1923